THE
BARN BOOK

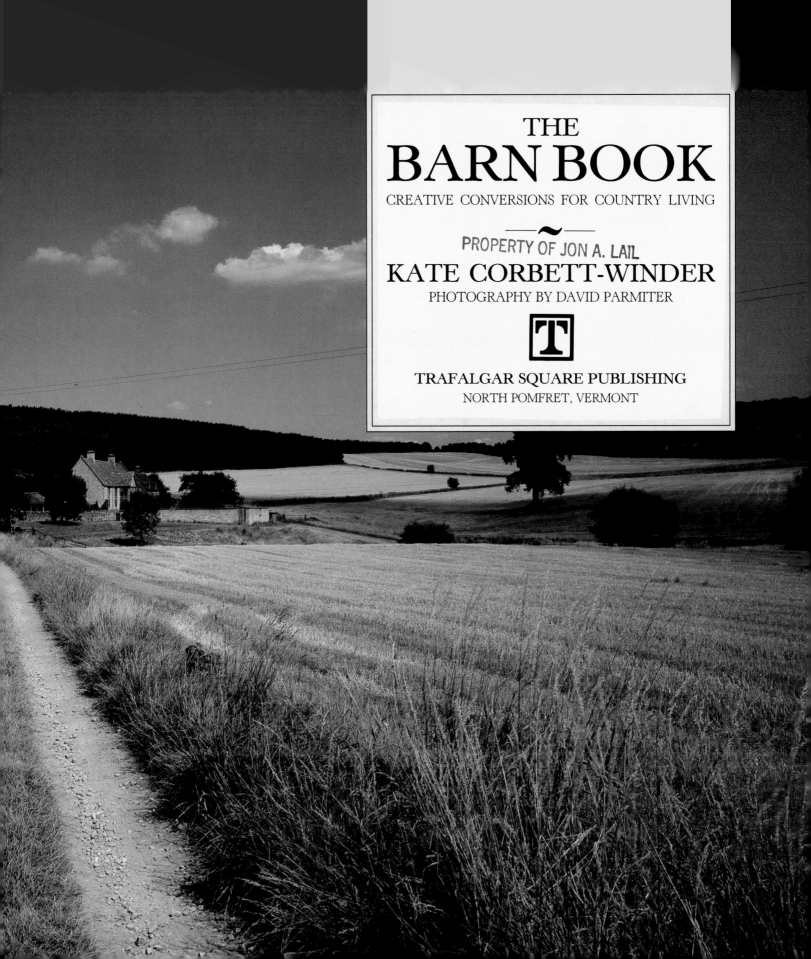

THE
BARN BOOK

CREATIVE CONVERSIONS FOR COUNTRY LIVING

~

KATE CORBETT-WINDER

PHOTOGRAPHY BY DAVID PARMITER

T

TRAFALGAR SQUARE PUBLISHING

NORTH POMFRET, VERMONT

BY THE SAME AUTHOR:

Vogue More Dash Than Cash

Vogue Even More Dash Than Cash

First published in the United States of America in 1990
by Trafalgar Square Publishing, North Pomfret,
Vermont 05053

ISBN: 0-943955-28-9

LOC: 90-70063

Designed by Nigel Partridge

Shawls and tie-back for front cover photography kindly
supplied by The Gallery of Antique Costume and Textiles,
2 Church Street, London NW8

Set in Horley Old Style by SX Composing Ltd

Printed and bound in Singapore by Toppan Printing
Company

CONTENTS

—~—

For my mother

ACKNOWLEDGEMENTS

I would like to thank the owners of the buildings in *The Barn Book* for all their help, enthusiasm and hospitality; Huw Thomas for his architectural advice and interest; my husband William and children Willow, Ned and Tom who were abandoned while I searched the country for suitable buildings; my mother who helped me to finish the book on time, and my sister Anna Hogg who drove, map read and kept me company for many long miles.

INTRODUCTION

—⁀—

Barns have been a part of the landscape since the middle ages, as significant as the village church or manor house. Their simple architecture punctuates the countryside, giving a picture of rural history and tradition that distinguishes one region from another. Traditional farm buildings display a long-standing harmony with their surroundings, giving each part a particular identity. How bleak the Cotswolds or Yorkshire Dales would look without weathered stone barns, or Hereford-shire without its distinctive timber-framed buildings. They are not just characteristic landmarks. They represent the pattern of local agriculture and indigenous materials, built in a shape and scale that suited their function.

But modern farming no longer fits the form of its Victorian predecessors. As methods become more mechanized and intensive, the number of redundant barns increases – old buildings that are incompatible with late twentieth-century machines. Until the architectural and heritage value of farm buildings was recognized in the early 1980s, a tragic number were demolished to make way for standard tin sheds – low in maintenance costs and character – but cavernous enough for modern combine harvesters, tractors and grain driers. Grants were available for new buildings, but for old and increasingly obsolete buildings there was no financial aid. The solution was to sell them and, as the idea of conversion caught on, it was an increasingly lucrative one.

There are vehemently opposing camps that question the future of farm buildings. But, as this book aims to prove, a sympathetic balance can be struck between the strict conservationists, who prefer letting forgotten buildings crumble quietly in the landscape, and the astute property developer who sees a redundant farmyard as a potential housing complex. The recent spate of barn conversions has drawn attention to the disastrous travesties that resemble oversized bungalows trimmed with suburban detail. These monstrosities are an alien breed compared with the sensitive buildings that do exist around the country, personally restored by their owners employing traditional methods and materials that merge into the landscape.

The barns, stables and granaries featured in this book were all empty, threatened or derelict. Their future has been salvaged by conversion into original, often eccentric homes that retain a strong character and sense of the past. Many of the owners are architects, designers and artists whose imaginations and energies have been challenged by the possibilities of a dark stone cowshed, a circular hop kiln or a Palladian stable block.

The book's emphasis on conversions in the south of England and the Midlands reflects different regional pressures. The quantity of redundant farm buildings in agricultural counties such as East Anglia, Hampshire, Wiltshire and Gloucester-shire provide an answer to the demand for housing on the edge of a village. Further north, where farms are smaller, many traditional buildings are still in working use. Others are abandoned in remote parts of the country where planning controls prevent conversion and their distance from a village makes electricity and water supplies an impractical proposition. Now that planning laws forbid anyone to build an isolated country house, a barn can be an unusual alternative offering spacious proportions on a grand scale, a rural setting and historic background. It offers the freedom, unstamped by human occupation, for a spectacular living space.

The most successful conversions give an impression of minimal change. They respect the original function and character of the building, transforming a disintegrating shell into a warm, solid structure with faithful attention to regional detail. The use of appropriate old tiles, slates, timbers and stones gives a settled look to the renovation. For it to become a conventional house, a barn must lose its personality. For a barn *does* have a personality and to segment it into snug-sized rooms will certainly destroy it. Barns are only for people who like the feeling of open space.

The style of conversion depends entirely on the age and type of a building. A tithe barn with a sweeping tiled roof has a contrasting scale and atmosphere to an upland bank barn or one of a cruck-framed construction. Yet there is a recognizable pattern to eighteenth- and nineteenth-century barns built for storing and processing crops during the agricultural boom that occurred between 1750 and 1870. Known abroad as the English Barn, they are tall elongated buildings divided into three or more bays, with a central threshing floor flanked by high doors through which wagons brought in sheaves of corn to be threshed and winnowed during the winter.

The glory of these barns is their awe-inspiring volume of space, disturbed only by a hayloft at one end, and vertical posts, braces and roof trusses between the bays. But adapting such an area for everyday living can present a conflict between practical and conservation priorities. Many are listed buildings which means that, although planning permission is more likely to be granted, they are constrained by strict regulations designed to safeguard their characteristic features. Some local authorities recommend that as much as two-thirds of the ground to roof height is left intact. Others insist that no structural load be added to the barn framework so that, in theory, a domestic intrusion could be dismantled and the barn taken back into agricultural use.

The logical and only feasible approach is to work around the existing structure, rather than battle against beams that dissect the barn in awkward places. As the roof has such a powerful effect on the character and scale of a barn interior, it is criminal to hide it away in upstairs bedrooms slotted between the trusses. Where a living room spanning the full ground to ridge height feels too cavernous, the alternative may be an upper galleried sitting room that overlooks the central volume of space. As such airiness is more inviting in summer than winter, a barn does need to have one cosy manageable area – a comfortable kitchen or living room – warmed by an Aga or open fire.

An alternative to the open acres of storage bays and threshing floors is found inside a combination barn. Here a cowhouse, stable, hayloft, granary and cartshed were contained under one roof, often forming an L-shape around a modest farmyard. The different sections suggest a sequence of rooms on two floors, with bedrooms in the hayloft and granary and living rooms below in the stables, cowhouse and cartshed. The appearance of stable blocks is less predictable than with other farm buildings. Horses kept for sporting purposes on country estates often had grander accommodation in architect-designed stables that echoed their parent house. As a valuable part of the workforce, farm horses were treated with consideration. Unlike cows kept in low dark sheds, horses lived in generous stalls separated by tall wooden partitions (that prevented them from seeing each other), below high ceilings that allowed plenty of fresh air to circulate.

Retaining the traditional hallmarks of a building helps to emphasize its agricultural past. The strongest architectural features – the barn or stable doors, the plain sweep of the roof, the timber-framed walls – need to dominate without being upstaged by domestic essentials. Incorporating some of the original elements gives the interior a rustic authenticity. Depending on their condition, the flagstones or cobbles from the threshing floor may be relaid inside or out; vertical oak posts and beams can be used as in-built supports for climbing plants or shelves for books and ornaments. Wooden mangers in cowsheds, stables and the panelled walls of a tack room can endorse the rustic spirit of the building.

The balance of creating a home without diluting its agricultural origins can be helped by the building's position. If the north side faces outward on to a road or village it is logical to keep the agricultural front with its discreet ventilation slits and traditional boarded entrance on public view, allowing larger windows and glazed doors to open on to a south-facing garden.

Although the least conspicuous conversions suggest an almost primitive simplicity, many are packed with sophisticated technology. Taking a building apart provides an opportunity to install complete insulation, under-floor heating, thermostatic glazing, in-built music systems, wine cellars, even sound-proofed walls. Other necessities are impossible to hide. All houses need doors, windows and chimneys, which should blend carefully into the building without broadcasting its change of use too loudly. Extra daylight is an essential addition, usually governed by building regulations that insist on keeping the original openings, at least on the public side of a building. Because barns and cowsheds seldom had conventional windows, there is no precedent to follow. The style of window becomes an issue of personal choice negotiated between the owner, architect and local planning authority, which if inappropriate can distort the whole appearance, giving a curious hybrid look. At first impression, the less conspicuous they are the better.

At ground level extra light can be introduced by expanding the ventilation slits into long narrow windows and by glazing the barn doors or side walls of a gabled porch. The least obtrusive windows are set without frames straight into the walls or slotted between the panelling as glass 'nogging' in a timber framework. Lighting the upper level of a barn can be more difficult, especially where a wide roof sweeps right down to low eaves. Skylights may not disturb the roofline but they are immediately obvious, glinting in the sun from a distance. Usually the best compromise is to leave the outward view intact and make changes to the inward side. Small dormer windows are more prominent but less blatantly modern, although as some late nineteenth-century barns did have skylights they could be considered more authentic. Yet dormers appear more sympathetic to traditional architecture, echoing the pitch of a gabled porch and adding an hospitable expression to a blank roof. Gable end walls often have a ready-made window space in the pitching hole – a high entrance used for loading hay into the loft. Where extra light is needed, a triangular chunk between the eaves could be glazed, catching the evening sun on a west-facing wall.

Chimneys are another sign of human occupation but they need not detract from a traditional appearance. Some planning authorities recommend an industrial flue instead of a brick or stone chimney but, as a rural barn is hardly an industrial building, why make it look urban with a metal flue pipe, however slender? A low stone or brick chimney on the domestic side of the roof need not look too conspicuous, especially if it is set well below the ridge.

The immediate surroundings have an important effect on the whole appearance. Land around a derelict building invariably deteriorates into a ragged wilderness which is then buried beneath rubble and debris during the conversion process. Taming or bulldozing it into a garden is the final challenge, requiring as much sensitivity as the building work. As there is no original plan to follow or restore, its design needs to be in harmony with the surrounding countryside. Natural planting should connect the building to the landscape, encouraging indigenous flowers and trees to suggest that they have always grown there. Anything contrived looks incongruous beside an agricultural façade.

There is no escaping the expense of conversion. It is far cheaper and less complicated to build a new house than resurrect an uncompromising old barn or cowshed. But as there is seldom the same rapport between new houses and their surroundings – and their owners – it seems entirely logical to save these redundant buildings and keep the tradition of vernacular architecture alive. This book is not intended as a practical guide, more an inspirational insight into a rustic way of life that can preserve a vulnerable part of our rural heritage.

MOAT HOUSE BARN

KATE AND DAVID BUCKETT

Moat House Barn has a strong sense of the past. True to its name, it stands surrounded by water on a site once occupied by the Bishop of Winchester's country retreat. Here, secluded from the medieval world outside, the Bishop kept five monks in a chantry at constant prayer for his soul. Part of the retreat was a farm settlement where, according to accounts that date back to 1208, corn from the Bishop's estates was stored. Most of the medieval buildings were destroyed during the Dis-

solution of the Monasteries, but some of the original brick, flint and masonry survived and were recycled into a sixteenth-century manor house and adjoining barn. Both are buildings on a grand scale that reflect the prosperity of this Hampshire estate. The barn has the soaring proportions of an ecclesiastical tithe barn but was used to thresh, winnow and store grain from the home farm.

When David Buckett discovered it seven years ago, all sense

BELOW, *Before conversion; after disintegrating for years surrounded by a concrete farmyard, Moat House Barn needed serious renovation. David Buckett was to do much of the conversion work himself.*

RIGHT, *The gable end of the barn was completely bowed and rebuilt with old, weathered bricks that matched the original walls. Steps from the garden lead up to a terrace along the glass wall of the living room.*

of history had been invaded by farm buildings crowded into a concrete yard. Now their only trace is the odd iron post camouflaged in a garden between the barn and a high medieval wall. Although Moat House Barn has been converted, it is still unquestionably a barn. Gigantic oak beams, braces and vertical posts dominate as they have done for centuries. Their massive size and quality are permanent reminders of their age and pedigree – the older the barn, the bigger the beam. The dirt floor, ventilation slits and transverse cart doors have all been altered, but the grand scale remains.

The exterior has been restored, radically in parts, with old materials that give a settled, timeworn look. The tiled roof sweeping down to low eaves blends with the random stone, flint, brickwork and natural oak window frames set deep into the walls. One reason for the success of Moat House Barn lies with the likemindedness of David Buckett and his architect, Huw Thomas. As pioneers of barn conversion, both wanted to retain all the history and character of the building. 'The idea is that even though it's a house, the barn still dominates,' explains Huw. Moat House Barn was their first joint project which won an award from the Country Landowners Association and led to commissions for similar conversions all over the country.

Although the timbers were solid, their surrounding structure was weak. The barn had been left to deteriorate for five years before David bought it. Both gable ends were disintegrating, further threatened by

LEFT, In the upstairs bathroom, a delicately stencilled bath perches under the slope of a massive oak brace

BELOW, The flagstoned entrance leads up a flight of stairs to the living room or down steps past the lily pond to the dining hall

the dismantling of a concrete milking parlour at one end of the barn. The wall was saved by a metal rod and tie beam, but the opposite gable end was bowed and had to be completely rebuilt with old red bricks. From the start there was to be nothing conventional about the project. David was to do much of the building work himself and supported any plan that preserved the barn spirit. Huw's approach was an upside-down arrangement of a living room on the first floor and bedrooms below. 'It's such a mistake to egg crate the whole top floor and try to squeeze bedrooms around the beams.'

There was enough height in the barn to put in a suspended floor for a large galleried sitting room where the full glory of the roof could reign. At ground level, where corn was once threshed and winnowed, a central dining hall spans the full height of the barn. It recalls a seventeenth-century pattern of the first floor *piano nobile* approached by a sweeping staircase. Here the staircase is T-shaped, inspired by a flight in St David's Cathedral in Cardiff. It opens on to a narrow catwalk that leads in one direction to a sitting room, and in the other to a bathroom and three bedrooms. A clever entrance encourages you to climb to an upper living space. The front door remains in its original place but the level has been raised so you arrive almost midway between the ground and the first floor. This gives an immediate impression of the barn as one open space and as you are facing the stairs, it seems logical to go on up.

One drawback of an upper

living room was the lack of daylight. The original ventilation slits in the rebuilt gable end were expanded into arched windows and a giant glass triangle fitted between the eaves, but it was still not enough to lighten the top floor. Because the barn was semi-detached and overlooked a neighbour's garden, the opposite end could not be glazed. The solution – a shock to some barn purists – was to cut an oblong chunk out of the roof so that glass could be fitted right along the wall of the room. It does interrupt the tiled sweep, but avoids the intrusion of skylights which are an anathema to Huw and David. Their idea caused a battle between the architect and planning officer, especially as legislation for barn conversion had not yet been specified. 'There is always a conflict between the conservation mind and the designer, but you *can* make it a house and keep the dignity of the barn. At the end of the day, you are saving the building,' insists Huw. It was not too much of a liberty. The cut did not threaten the original fabric; the south-facing aisle was a Victorian addition, built with softwood, rather than oak. The glass wall opens on to a narrow terrace filled with plants that, from below, seem to sprout from the lower roof top.

The interior has been designed by Kate Buckett who married David and his barn soon after he had moved in. It changed gradually from bachelor to family home for their sons, Tom, Leo and Jack. In the sitting room a robust framework of wood, brick and white paint between open rafters creates such visual impact that elaborate furnishings are unnecessary. Some beams are dressed with a nonchalant loop of fabric. Apart from these, there is an intentional lack of curtains. A red-brick fire surround slotted between sloping braces gives a focus to the seating area, furnished with two substantial sofas, an armchair and a long, low table sliced from a spare beam. Against all the biscuity oak, added colour is achieved with clear pastel tones – sage, coral, turquoise – brightened with jungle-sized plants.

Even with an open fire, insulated roof and central heating, the sitting room is not exactly intimate. To compensate, the barn is designed for summer and winter living. Summer is spent upstairs and winter downstairs in a cosier kitchen-cum-parlour that leads off the dining hall. Once the milking

parlour, it is now a multi-purpose family room where children and parents spend a great deal of time – cooking, eating, playing and relaxing.

Apart from practical considerations of heating, open-plan living is not baby or childproof. Some of David's original ideas have had to be modified to suit small children. A raised stone pond in the hall is filled with toys and plants instead of the water and floating lilies he had imagined. House rules forbid the children to go upstairs alone so they sleep downstairs below the sitting room. Kate and David have a bedroom with connecting bathroom opposite, decorated in pale green with a mural painted by Kate to match an Oriental wall hanging. When family life allows, she works as a graphic artist in a tiny upstairs studio tucked between the eaves.

Nowhere has convenience detracted from the barn spirit. There is a deliberate simplicity to the decorative style and finish. The hall and dining space are paved with York flagstones; the kitchen, bathroom and master bedroom with unpolished Spanish marble. The oak beams have been left as raw and textured as possible. To keep their paleness, they were washed with high pressure water jets. 'Sandblasting is too abrasive and would have destroyed the natural colour,' explains David. 'That pale surface is only skin deep. If you clean away too much, the oak goes dark.' You could not be too houseproud in Moat House Barn – dust is a permanent feature along the tops of beams. 'It is a Forth Bridge job trying to keep them clean,' says Kate. But the beams make useful in-built shelves, housing plants, birdcages – also filled with plants – and a pair of stuffed alligators that watch over the sitting room. At ground level the posts, like rustic columns, are entwined with greenery climbing from terracotta pots.

At night the theatrical atmosphere increases, especially when the central bay becomes a dining hall, open to the rafters. Uncurtained glass doors behind the refectory table act like giant mirrors, heightening the sense of space with dramatic reflections. The table is lit from above by ecclesiastical candles burning in an iron chandelier made from an old cartwheel. Furniture throughout the barn is eclectic but matched to the

The dining hall in the central threshing bay reveals the barn's soaring height; proportions matched by a long oak table, jungle-sized plants and an unobtrusive snakeskin

scale and slightly larger than life atmosphere. Carved oak shelves salvaged from the first-class bar of the *Mauretania* occupy one kitchen wall; the other is consumed by a massive pine dresser, partly dismantled into kitchen units. These are topped with ancient Jurassic tiles from Germany, embedded with pre-historic fossils.

Outside, Kate has created a traditional English garden, contained by the original moat and capped medieval wall. There is

The Bucketts' winter quarters lead off the dining hall. Here comfort and cosier dimensions make an all-purpose kitchen, playroom and sitting room for children and grown-ups.

now a lawn in place of five layers of concrete. David traded the rubble with a farmer in exchange for the underlying soil. He then raised the garden height, levelling it for a grass tennis court. It is edged with herbaceous borders full of pink and white perennials and shrubs. Kate keeps to roses, phloxes, daisies – avoiding August's hot-coloured chrysanthemums or dahlias. Her garden also climbs the barn walls, hidden in high summer behind a mass of sweet peas that nudge the eaves.

STEPPES MILL HOUSE

ANN AND NIGEL WALSH

~

What could be more quaintly olde worlde to an American than a real English cider house? After living in New Jersey for ten years, Ann and Nigel Walsh felt a strong yearning for a share of rustic tradition. On their return to England they house-hunted intensively for three months, looking at up to six houses a day until they found Steppes Mill House in Herefordshire. It consisted of two detached buildings, linked by the previous owner into one house. The older half was a sixteenth-century cider house, in working order until the early 1900s. Beside it stood a substantial stone cottage built 200 years later where the miller and family lived, running their cider farm and smallholding. Both parts had been joined into a manageable family house – not too large for two people but large enough for children and grandchildren – with a kitchen, dining room and sitting room in the cider house and bedrooms and bathrooms in the cottage.

The conversion was designed by Martin Opie, an architect from Hereford, who bought the derelict building and restored it for himself. He took on a leaking stone and timber-framed structure two storeys high – a potential living space that needed a new roof, extra windows and some interior rearrangement. A large share of the ground floor in the living area was taken up by the cider mill, consisting of a round stone trough – 'the bedstone' where the apples were ground to a pulp by a horsedrawn stone wheel. The cider maker would walk in circles behind the horse, adding apples to the mill and scraping pulp from the side of the trough. Once a layer of

The old cider press is decked with geraniums instead of a 'cheese' of apple pulp. In the loft a random pattern of windows replace the brick nogging between the timber framework.

apples had been crushed, a bucket of water was thrown in to stop the mixture getting too sticky.

Today, the redundant cider mill still in its original position is put to an alternative use. As an in-built fixture it makes an original storage and display area, like a circular mantelpiece. A detachable wooden lid for the trough provides extra seating which is removed in autumn to make way for the apple harvest – part edible, part decorative. At Christmas the trough brims with festive red apples that scent the air and give colour to the room. Somehow Ann plans to find space to display an old saddle, harness and blinkers, left behind in the cellar.

When in working order, the cider press would have been kept inside next to the mill. Now it stands outside like a giant oak vice with a protruding rusty nail. Originally, it would have pressed a 'cheese' of apple pulp piled between horse-hair cloths, left to steep until all the juice had been extracted and the 'cheese' reduced to a third of its height. The cider was then left to ferment in large wooden casks. When the Walshes arrived they discovered an anonymous vat of alcohol. Rather than cider, it turned out to be well-matured apple wine, as potent as sherry.

Inside the mill there is an atmosphere of perpetual harvest festival. Oak posts and ceiling joists are festooned with home-grown hops, dried flowers, grasses and mistletoe. Beneath their decoration the oak joists look centuries old but were installed during the conversion to divide the open space in two. The low ceiling gives an immediate cosiness to the room with its simple white stone walls and brick floor – an essential foil to the rustic profusion and an appropriate setting for the Laura Ashley furnishings and faded Turkish rugs. 'You can't have anything too fussy in here,' says Ann. 'It's a deliberate choice not to have any curtains.' A new stone wall has been built behind the cider mill, separating the kitchen and dining area, although they are still connected through an open hatch.

A steep staircase leads to the first floor – an extension of the small loft where apples were stored in a corner of the cider house. Now used as a sitting room, it extends right over the ground floor. As the only windows were at ground level extra light was essential on the first floor. Instead of rebricking all the timber-based panels as before, some were left open and turned into windows, dotted between floor and roof height. Their random pattern adds to the eccentric exterior

and creates an airy upstairs sitting room. Additional light comes through windows set into the far ridge of the roof, a scheme that leaves an unbroken tiled sweep at the front. Central heating is backed up by a woodburning stove and there is cork insulation between the rafters. Downstairs, the original oak window frames are sealed with Sellotape to help exclude the Herefordshire draughts. Warmth is essential in a place like this.

A tiny conservatory added at the far end of the dining room brings a garden element inside. It looks on to an orchard of cider apple trees where the fallen fruit lies rotting in the grass through the winter months. 'They are iron hard and useless for cooking,' explains Ann. On such a smallholding pigs would have rootled, feasting on windfalls or the dry 'pomace' pulp left from the pressings. Sadly, their sties crumbled to ruins long years ago.

ABOVE, *The sitting room extended from the apple loft remains partitioned by a wattle panel*

RIGHT, *Each autumn apples fill the stone trough and home-grown hops and flowers festoon the beams*

COB HOUSE

JOHN AND ELIZABETH FALCONER

~

'In the very sump of the valley wallowed the Squire's Big House – once a fine, though modest sixteenth-century manor, to which a Georgian façade had been added.' This is Laurie Lee's fitting description of Steanbridge House in *Cider with Rosie*. There is no mention of the stable block built at the same time as the Georgian façade by the horse-loving squire, Mr Townsend. Having grandified the manor in 1780, his architect turned his skills to a superior stable block, creating a Palladian building in pale Cotswold stone with a symmetrical façade of arched windows above the stalls and mangers.

Two hundred years later the stables were less impressive. They were empty and derelict, but an inviting proposition to architect John Falconer and his artist wife, Elizabeth. Their original plan had been to share the big house bought by their son Toby, but the stables, rechristened Cob House, were more appealing. At the time, the Falconers were living in a Cotswold barn, plotting their next home. John's ideal was a Palladian villa in Tuscany, Elizabeth's an unconverted mill. A Palladian stable block was a perfect compromise, especially when John promised to dig a large mill pond in front.

Although the building was structurally in good order, inside it was chaotic, as if the horses had bolted 50 years before, leaving black runnelled floors, trails of hay, muck and shattered windows. But the chaos was super-ficial. Beneath lay the frame for a spacious airy ground floor with a central hall flanked by two large living rooms. The hay-loft above consisted of small basic rooms leading off a long pas-sage overlooking the back yard. Upstairs, apart from plumbing in two bathrooms, it was a case of basic renovation and dec-orating. Downstairs needed far more serious attention.

Introducing extra light into the long, dark stalls was the most urgent step, achieved by replacing the blind stone win-dow set below each glass arch with wide sash frames. Today both living rooms are filled with light flooding through three full-height windows topped by their original fan-lights. A new half-glass front door replaced the solid one, brightening the hall and stair-case. The façade full of win-dows gives Cob House the air of an orangery, accentuated by a vigorous clematis, honey-suckle and roses that have covered the walls in five years. The south-facing windows along the front all open on to a wide stone terrace crowded with plants beside Elizabeth's mill pond. Beyond the garden, steep wooded valleys rise to the skyline.

While the conversion was in progress the Falconers lived in a cottage next door, close enough to chivvy the builders from October to February, when the stables became just about habitable. As architect and artist, both had a strong

An arched window at the top of the stairs replaces a door into the hay loft. Its stone sill makes a peaceful place to survey the pond and garden below.

practical and visual sense of what was to be done. A specialist in converted buildings, John is sensitive to danger areas, parti-cularly windows and chimneys, which can shout out the change of use. 'It is important to remember what the building was used for originally; alterations must be simple and straight-forward,' he says. Besides the reinstatement of windows, an obvious addition to Cob House was a second chimney for a fireplace in one of the living rooms. It adds an appropriate balance to the building, under-lining its Palladian symmetry.

Having lightened the in-teriors, the proportions were perfect with high beamed ceil-ings balanced by the length and breadth of both rooms. Their volume is emphasized by a smaller scale hall in the tack room. Here the ceiling was lowered as a contrast and to heighten the landing above. Sadly, the tack room panelling was stripped from the walls and discarded in the snow by zealous builders before Eliza-beth could recycle it. The old fireplace remains but the stair-case had to be rebuilt, follow-ing the curve of the original. Threats of rising ammonia from years of ingrained horse manure proved to be un-founded. After laying a damp course and replastering there have been no reprisals – apart from a few cracks in the wall caused by the central heating.

Although the ground floor is divided between three rooms, they have a strong continuity, linked by a honey-coloured

stone floor, white walls and calm decoration – a suggestion of French provençal crossed with African ethnic. The living room combines an informal sitting room, dining space and kitchen, answering the Falconers' need for one large room where they can cook, eat, relax, watch television or listen to music. A giant stone fireplace dominates one end, the dining table and chairs are central and the kitchen, partly obscured by

The white walls, stone floors and brown papered ceiling lend a neutral background to the Falconers' living room – a generous space of perfect proportions

a dresser and tall shelving, occupies the far end. Like so much in the house, the fireplace is of French inspiration. After a spring holiday in a Dordogne farmhouse with an efficient open fire, Elizabeth made working drawings and repeated the exact design at Cob House. The secret of its tremendous draught is a long thin slit, 2 feet by 6 inches at the tip of the flue. 'We had to talk our way round building regulations but now, to the rage of our neighbours, we have a fire in the valley that doesn't smoke!' says Elizabeth. Beside the fireplace stand two low sofas. One is more like a bed covered with a Kenyan carpet and bank of kilim cushions – possessions brought back from years in East Africa where John designed a cathedral and leprosy centre for the Catholic Mission.

White walls and pale oatmeal curtains make a neutral background for the substantial, yet uncluttered contents; a personal collection of country antiques, ethnic textiles, silver-framed etchings, baskets of logs, magazines in neat piles on the stone floor. The Falconers' taste is fixed, 'any colour as long as it's white,' insists Elizabeth, 'but I do like to have colour in the rugs and furnishings – it's what my children call ghastly good taste.' The ceiling treatment adds a warm cigar box effect to the room. Space between the new oak joists has been lined with brown wrapping paper – an idea borrowed from David Hicks after John worked with him on a London house. It reflects the stone floor and flatters the bleached wooden furniture painted by Elizabeth. She uses a special glaze and recipe learnt years ago from an American decorator that gives the hemlock dining table and pine dresser a pickled timeworn look.

The kitchen is a compact oblong space lined with pine shelves, cupboards, blue-and-white tiled worksurfaces and dark-green Aga. Both John and Elizabeth are keen cooks, particularly of French and traditional English food. In summer, a fortuitous walnut tree in the garden casts shade over the cooking area, cooling the heat of the Aga. Both the terrace and interior floors are laid with smooth squares of modern Beckston concrete, made from the dust of local stone pulverized at Burford quarry. 'The secret is not to treat them,' explains Elizabeth, 'to let dogs and gumboots give them a battered look.'

The dimensions of the drawing room are a mirror image of the living room. One half has been requisitioned by John as an airy work place, away from his Cheltenham office. The other half has a more formal quality than the multi-purpose room across the hall, dominated by an identical French-inspired stone hearth that backs on to the hall fireplace. Its scale is balanced by two of Elizabeth's large unframed portraits. After moving from London to the country she changed direction from painting to illustrating children's books. Her finely detailed pictures of animals, children and natural history reflect a decorative flair that pervades the house and garden.

Upstairs there is a tranquillity that spreads from the central landing; a spare, uncluttered space dominated by a tall arched window – replacing a door used to load hay into the loft. The deep stone sill makes a peaceful place to watch trout darting in the pond below, guarded from predators by a decoy heron. Deliberate changes in floor level, rather than strong decoration, add to the character. Steps both sides of the landing lead to a passage of bedrooms – all with white walls, dark-green carpet and sea-blue doors with porcelain knobs. Apart from a lofty master bedroom where elm beams trace the hipped roof, the bedrooms and bathroom are small with sloping ceilings and floor-level windows.

As passionate Francophiles they had plans to buy a holiday home in the south of France. But the pressure of work and John's health prompted a permanent holiday element at Cob House instead. They built an indoor swimming pool hidden in a conservatory behind the hall. Dug out of a hill at the back of the stables, it is impeccably built in glass and old bricks that match the high garden wall.

In front of Cob House there is a tangible calm, generated by the mill pond and surrounding garden. It is laid out in a quiet architectural style, influenced by Sissinghurst and Hidcote. 'I love a no-colour garden, just greys, greens, white flowers, perhaps a few blue geraniums, and of course, water,' says Elizabeth. 'I actually prefer it in winter when the place looks dim and watery.' Mature shrubs and herbaceous plants thrive in borders and pots along the stone terrace, wafting their scent through open windows. Silver-grey senecios and artemisias grow among old-fashioned roses and more modern species – creamy Iceberg and silvery pink New Dawn – that extend the flowering season. Beyond the pond an Ellwood cypress hedge grows to conceal a row of cottages. And inspired by the gardens at Hidcote, Elizabeth is planning to trim these trees into a slope that follows the cottage roofline.

Upstairs, decoration is kept plain and simple. In John and Elizabeth's bedroom, a bold Indian quilt reflects the network of beams across the high hipped roof.

CHALK BARN
JENNY AND MIKE ADAMS

—~—

Jenny Adams grew up beside Chalk Barn; an early Victorian stable, granary and barn on her father's farm in Hampshire. When the land was divided between her brothers, Jenny inherited the barn and decided to convert it into a family house with her husband Mike. Chalk Barn is L-shaped with a deep slate roof. It was no architectural beauty but the combination of space and manageable proportions had great potential. The building was unlisted so it took all of Jenny's exuberant personality, and the persistence of her architect, to persuade the local planners for permission to preserve an increasingly rare species of chalk barn. Unless rendered regularly, the chalk and then the building gradually deteriorate.

Luckily, Jenny's barn was caught in time. It needed re-rendering and re-roofing but the structure of the whole building was sound. Like a blank canvas it was an empty shell that could be organized around the needs of a family with four young children. The result, which spreads through the stables, granary and barn, is an original and efficient house, punctuated by deliberate changes in floor level. It feels more contemporary than rustic. The beams appear to be incidental, rather than focal points that dictated the dimensions of rooms. The front of the stables and granary beside the road has been given a necessary face-lift; the corrugated tin entrance was replaced with a solid arched door; narrow ventilation slits were widened into evenly spaced window arches with red-brick reveals that match those of a neighbouring Victorian cottage. As this side faces north, it contains the practical rooms; kitchen, landing, utility room and lavatory, while the living rooms and bedrooms face south into the privacy of a garden and gentle countryside beyond.

The barn, at right angles to the stables and granary, is the focal point of the house and has been converted into a vast drawing room and billiards room with a gallery at each end. It makes a perfect space for large scale entertaining but, in a family house, the day-to-day needs tend to be more mundane

The stables, granary and barn open onto a sheltered garden that is climbing the chalk walls. Perhaps one day the plants will grow tall enough to hide the stains of apple-hurling contests against the barn.

ABOVE, *Green against green; billiards dominate the other half of the barn, played at ground level or watched from above*

LEFT, *In the drawing-room end of the barn, comfortable sofas are overlooked by a cider press and toy trains in the minstrels' gallery*

and take priority. With these in mind, Chalk Barn has been designed for both child-orientated and grown-up lifestyles. The grown-up zone, consisting of the barn, the guest bedroom and bathroom, are away from the hub of the house and can be closed off, leaving the kitchen, dining room, sitting room, upstairs bedrooms and bathrooms as an everyday zone. As so much of family life revolves around the kitchen, it seemed logical to have a room that is large enough for the children, nanny, parents and friends to talk, cook, eat and play all at the same time.

The room divides in two but keeps an open-plan feeling. The kitchen side occupies the old carthorse stables, where a new ceiling gives cosier proportions than the original height from ground to rafters. It has a polished, country atmosphere, full of rustic textures; a quarry-tiled floor, dark-green painted cupboards, brick and wooden worktops, mounted on a saddle-stone plinth. This was recycled from the old granary where it kept grain out of the reach of rats. Steps from the kitchen lead into a larger dining area converted from the granary. As the ground level was originally only dimly lit by narrow ventilation holes, it needed much more daylight. So a massive chunk of brickwork was cut out of the south-facing wall and replaced with French windows that open on to a wide paved terrace.

Jenny realized the risks involved in the partial demolition of such a major wall and was very grateful to her user-friendly builders. 'We didn't employ one firm but used a nucleus of local workmen. A large firm would have charged a fortune to cover themselves for all the eventualities.' In fact, the set-backs were minimal and the whole process took only nine months to complete. The advantage of collaborating closely with her architect and builders – and also doing much of the work herself - was being able to plan and change things as they went along. 'It's the only way to work on a project like this,' Jenny insists.

Jenny's initial preference for a low-maintenance interior without bare stone or wooden floors altered as the barn progressed. 'Somehow once we'd started, it had to be full of natural things,' she explains. Apart from the quarry-tiled kitchen, the floors are laid with pine roofing boards salvaged from a Southampton hospital by a resourceful builder. The oriental carpets and kilims add warmth and colour to the white paint and pine that dominate the interior. The dining space is rustic but bright, furnished with a long pine table, country chairs, a pine dresser and large mirrors. Red cotton lampshades, plants, dried flowers and the inevitable children's clutter give it an informal, family atmosphere. The French windows are left uncurtained which seems to link the interior and garden, especially in summer when the terrace becomes an alfresco dining room.

One of the most striking features of Chalk Barn are the substantial white walls, accentuated by expert plasterwork that curves round the corners and window recesses – a trick that brings more light into the rooms. The irregular wall contours also provide a natural shelving system to store plants, books and toys.

Upstairs, the space has been organized into compact bedrooms and bathrooms which open off an airy gallery landing. This makes an extra living space, furnished with a rocking chair, rugs and plants and lit by a skylight in the slope of the roof. A new partition wall between the landing and bedrooms appears quite authentic with lengths of old beams fitted into plasterboard panels.

Unlike the rest of the house where space is used conscientiously, the barn is an extravagant contrast. At first impression it is one vast room, a feeling that is emphasized by the volume from floor to roof, but it really contains four separate elements: a drawing room, billiards room and two minstrels' galleries tucked into each gable end – perfect vantage spots to watch billiards or eavesdrop on conversations below. A train set has taken priority over the anticipated library in the drawing-room gallery, but Jenny hopes it will evolve into a quiet place to read or study when the children are older. As the gable end faces south, a triangular window fitted across the end wall brings sunlight into the gallery and floor below. At ground level, a change in the floor height divides the two areas and adds to the scale of the barn. You walk into a carpeted billiards room then up two steps to a pine-floored drawing room where two large windows have replaced the old cart doors; one a French window that opens on to a stone terrace.

Confident that there was enough daylight in the barn, Jenny changed the walls from white to a deep, jade-green which instills a comfortable Georgian mood and lends a calm foil to the oak timbers. The furnishings have an appropriate elegance, comfortably defused by their rustic setting. Full length cream and copper moiré curtains rest in generous folds on the nut-brown floorboards. An Oriental carpet in front of the pine fireplace is flanked by two sofas that echo its soft colours, one a deep coral, the other a Chesterfield upholstered in eggshell-blue linen. A less formal arrangement of wicker armchairs faces the terrace in anticipation of summer beside terracotta pots trailing ivy and evergreens.

Standing in the middle of the barn is a large agricultural relic: a cider press which was found in pieces on a Somerset farm and reassembled for graceful retirement in Hampshire. It looks quite at home in its vernacular surroundings, if slightly incongruous beside the grass-green baize of the billiards table.

THE STABLES
IVOR AND CAROLINE WINDSOR-CLIVE

~

The Stables for Oakly Park in Shropshire date from the late eighteenth century, several decades before 1830 when their parent house was remodelled for Robert Clive, grandson of Clive of India. Now, instead of groomed horses and gleaming carriages, they are occupied by a direct descendant, Ivor Windsor-Clive, his wife Caroline and their children Robert, Freddy and India. More stately than rustic, the stables echo the grandeur of Cockerell's country house across the park. They stand at a dignified distance behind a walled courtyard with a drive of their own; a substantial E-shaped block topped with a central clock tower.

Until 1982 when Caroline stopped hunting, there were always horses in residence, stabled in one wing of the building. Carriages, stored in the opposite wing, were later replaced by farm vehicles and machinery. Above the stables there was a cavernous hayloft, reached by an outside ladder. Over the carriages there was basic accommodation for grooms and temporary estate workers – once occupied by Ivor's grandmother Lady Plymouth and family, who decamped to the grooms' quarters while Oakly Park was restored after army occupation during the Second World War. When Ivor took over the stables he planned to renovate the first-floor accommodation – two self-contained flats – as a weekend retreat from London. But after considering the size and quality of the building, Ivor, the architect and trustees decided there was potential for a more thorough conversion.

It has been a gradual twelve-year change from bachelor retreat to family house, expanding further into the building as more space was needed. After Robert was born, the hayloft became the nursery wing. The initial phase converted the middle section, the carriage store and floor above. A distressed combine harvester, rather than carriages, was parked behind massive doors in what is now the drawing room. Next door, now the dining room, was a dark fertilizer store. Before that it had been used to salt pigs. There has been no structural change to the outside of the stables – well-built with local Ludlow red brick and a sound slate roof – but the doors and windows needed rearranging. As Lord Plymouth wanted the building to retain its stable character, the original small-paned windows were kept and exact copies made for the new openings. The carriage doors in the drawing room were removed, the openings rebricked and fitted with three more windows to match the originals.

Inside, the poky entrance opening on to a rickety staircase needed to be given a sense of space. So now on arrival you walk through a square white-walled porch with a quarry-tiled floor into a hall that spans the front of the building. Turning right in the hall you come to the drawing room, a large oblong room lit by as many as six small-paned windows with deep low sills.

Ivor's initial 'sparse' decoration – rush matting, neutral tones, simple geometric wallpapers – has been softened by Caroline. The result is contemporary country house style rich in stripes and pastel linens, decorated more by texture than pattern. There is a noticeable lack of floral prints – just quantities of fresh and dried flowers arranged by Caroline.

To Ivor, the drawback of a converted building is the cramped proportions – especially if you are over six feet tall and a collector of modern British art. 'Unless you completely gut the place, you're never going to get the right proportions,' he says. The drawing

More stately than rustic, the stables for Oakly Park were built in the late eighteenth century, complete with a clock tower, walled courtyard and a drive of their own

room ceiling was raised slightly to provide more wall area for the large modern paintings, 'Although the spacing and height of the pictures doesn't really do them justice – you get a stamp-like effect.' The pale coral walls sponged by Caroline tone with cream linen curtains. A pair of sage-green four-seater sofas and two huge coral armchairs frame an exquisite Aubusson carpet – seating at least eight long-legged people in front of a white marble fireplace, salvaged from a local farmhouse.

The dining room next door has a persistent link with past occupants. Salt from years of pig preserving, followed by farm fertilizer has seeped into the fabric of the bricks and reappears after each coat of paint. The reaction of salt on the lining paper produces an instant distressed quality to the dragged red walls. 'It has a wonderfully Bacchanalian touch – as if it could have withstood the Hell Fire Club,' suggests Ivor. Three windows put into the dining room have striped, tomato cotton curtains from Pallu and Lake. They overlook a formal herb garden laid on the foundations of a dismantled outbuilding. Beyond stands a nineteenth-century barn with cladded oak walls. 'Apart from its unattractive tin roof, it stands out as 'a marvellous piece of Shropshire folk art,' says Ivor. Stacked with straw bales, it also makes an ideal summer playroom and site for children's picnics and parties in wet weather.

From the start, one of the stables' main attractions was an all-weather sporting arena – the walled courtyard laid with its original brick paviors. Sport is another of Ivor's passions: not the hunting or shooting associated with a Viscount but football, cricket or bowls. In winter, the garage doors of carriage proportions are flung open for a goal 'that almost meets FA regulations'. In summer, freestanding springback stumps are erected for stables cricket. 'We did use a dustbin as a wicket before but it's more aesthetically pleasing to have the real McCoy.' House rules means that everyone is involved – 'so no one has to go and pick daisies'.

While Ivor recruits children, nanny Hazel and friends, Caroline can retreat to her flower room converted from stalls in the stable quarters. The old partitions remain but all the woodwork and iron railings have been painted white and the floor relaid with chequerboard tiles. They make a striking backdrop to the profusion of dried rosebuds, peonies, larkspur, lavender and everlasting flowers arranged in baskets, bunches and swags, and potted trees – a small commercial enterprise, grown from a patch in the kitchen garden. The dried flowers overflow on to the kitchen ceiling. This is the only extension to the stables, added at the back of the building to replace a tiny kitchen behind the dining room.

The new room has transformed the atmosphere of the whole house, giving it an outlook and access to a terrace and informal garden. It provides an extra living space – 'a heart and soul to the stables,' explains Ivor – large enough for family, friends and extra children to congregate at a round table for an impromptu lunch. With no apparent effort Caroline will

LEFT, The primrose yellow kitchen connects the interior to the garden, creating a summery atmosphere, accentuated by the profusion of Caroline's flowers

BELOW, Bunches of dried hydrangeas, helichrysum and larkspur overflow onto a row of bells

rustle up a delicious cheese soufflé, home-grown salad and ice-cream. Even in winter the kitchen has a summery feel with primrose yellow walls, blue sofa and deck-chair-striped curtains. They frame tall sash windows that overlook the garden, stretching down to the River Teme. One opens on to a white fretwork balcony like a sentry post. Every inch of the wall space between white shelves and glass-fronted cupboards is crowded with contemporary paintings, most of them by Emma McClure.

Upstairs needed complete rearrangement into a compact plan of eight bedrooms and four bathrooms. 'The boys' bedrooms at one end of the hayloft are more like shoe boxes,' says Caroline. To compensate they have a vast airy playroom at the other end with a high beamed ceiling, white walls, cork floor and overflowing toy chests. The space has been partitioned at one side for a nursery kitchen and utility room which open through an arched hatch into the playroom. Instead of using the main hall, the children can make a quick exit down backstairs to the tack room, occupied by race tracks and train sets.

Ivor and Caroline's bedroom has the same rectangular proportions as the drawing room below. Not surprisingly, Caroline has redecorated, painting shell-pink over Ivor's textured blue wallpaper. The atmosphere is fresh and feminine, with a rush matting floor, dusty blue and pink linen chairs and Regency couch. Striped vanilla curtains – a variation of the dining room pattern – match the headboard and valance around the bed. Their adjoining bathroom and dressing room has an

Oriental style, papered with a Chinese print from Laura Ashley. From here a passage stencilled with faded oak leaves leads to a pair of connecting spare rooms, much used by families with children. The grown-ups sleep in a four-poster bed draped with sky-blue chintz, their children under patchwork quilts in pine truckle beds. A guest bathroom and further bedrooms open off the long putty-coloured landing laid with kilims. A desk and chair fitted into a niche above the porch make a tiny landing study for Caroline overlooking the courtyard through a window hung with Colefax and Fowler fuchsias. Ivor's study downstairs on the left of the hall has been usurped by the television. It is a small cosy room with enough space for a giant green sofa, reserved for serious sports viewing. 'We did have a small television in the drawing room, but they're such unattractive objects, we'd rather keep a huge one hidden away.'

Like the conversion, decoration has been done in gradual phases. Resisting the urge to take on everything at once has paid off. 'It's an advantage to live in a place and get the feel of it before you decorate,' believes Ivor. The hall is an example. After being white for six years, it was transformed by a Stilton cheese paint effect of blue veins marbled over a creamy ochre ground. It gives impact to the entrance yet blends with the honey-coloured oak floor staircase. Against the Stilton hangs a powerful pastoral scene of sheep and blossom by John Napper, a local artist and close friend, whose work appears on and in many walls. For, as well as featuring in framed form, he has sometimes mixed colours and painted the stable walls himself.

The dining room retains strong links with its past. The salt from years of pig preserving and sacks of fertilizer have seeped into the fabric of the wall, lending a distressed finish to the dragged red walls.

CHURCH BARN

BOB WEIGHTON

~

A pproaching Fotheringay across the River Nene you see a grand village church guarded from a respectable distance by a tall limestone barn. There is a great contrast in architecture but an obvious harmony between the buildings, as if bonded by age and history. Today Fotheringay is a peaceful Northamptonshire village, but 600 years ago it was a medieval capital surrounded by Rockingham Forest. Amid the royal hunt-

ing ground stood an impressive church, a college of priests and Fotheringay castle. The castle, given by Edward III to his younger son in 1337, was occupied by successive Dukes of York, by King Edward IV, the wives of Henry VIII and Mary Queen of Scots who was beheaded there in 1587. After being neglected in Tudor times, the castle, college and extensions to the church were demolished by James I, leaving only a mound beside the river as a remnant of the past.

Church Barn has its origins in the early history of Fotheringay, rebuilt in the late seventeenth century like much of the village with stone from the razed castle and college. Two adjacent barns with wide slate roofs form an L-shape with a long, low bullock pen which together flank the garden, once a burial ground for the lesser mortals of Fotheringay. Above it all, rising from the turreted church tower, the figure of a unicorn lifts its horn to the sky. When Bob Weighton began converting the barns in 1983 his builders unearthed recognizable human bones. Work stopped while archaeologists removed the contents of 15 graves, later identified by their burial positions as Saxon and medieval remains. After five years of analysis they were reburied in the churchyard, but the bones of one female aged between 14 and 17 which were discovered while the builders were digging out a floor, remain under the bullock pen wall. 'We thought it was kinder to leave her undisturbed,' explains Bob. 'We didn't want to be haunted, especially after watching the film *Poltergeist One!*'

Any lurking spirits are benevolent and lend a sympathetic atmosphere to the barn. It is a striking conversion, designed by its architect-owner, that works as a house without losing its identity as a farm building. The barn has two deliberate aspects. From the front one sees a discreet entrance within boarded cart doors and narrow slit windows. It presents a closed face that contrasts with the back where the architecture is more hospitable. Here glass set in the arched frame of the old cart doors gives a view inwards to the spacious dining room and outwards to the garden, paved terraces, flowerbeds and lawns. The sweep of the roof is interrupted by five dormer windows with white frames

that give a slightly quirky expression to the barn – as if raising its eyebrows. For Bob, dormer windows were a less intrusive idea than skylights. 'They look far more modern than little dormers collapsing into the roof at funny levels all over it. Also the dormers *could* have been there for a long time.'

Without losing the feel of space and volume, the overall aim was to create practical accommodation for Bob, his girlfriend Alex and her children Poppy and Sam. In its original state the large barn with its squared timbers was open to the roof, while the adjoining barn, the older of the two, was double-storeyed with a cobbled ground floor divided into sheep pens and a hayloft above supported by rafters formed from bundles of trees. Here the two floors have been retained but the large barn has been divided into three levels, juggling space in the roof for attic bedrooms. 'When the structure and raw materials are so simple and the spaces so good, you don't want to do anything clever that destroys the character of the building you started with,' says Bob. Although the space is divided, the natural textures and understated colours lead from room to room, one white geometric space linking another, patterned by oak joists, rafters and a restrained quantity of furniture. The arrangement of beams is a clever reworking of the original structure, giving an impression that little has changed but fitting three floors into the barn required some architectural expertise – and time. They were at it for a year.

Both buildings were in reasonable condition with limestone walls strong enough to support the extra floors without being underpinned, but at ground level the concrete cobbled floors had to be dug away to install a damp course and the slate roof, which replaced the thatch in the eighteenth century, needed some repair. A bullock pen at right angles to the larger barn serves a dual purpose as Bob's office and as a place for 'the gubbins of the house'. He explains, 'If you want to have open spaces without clutter, you've got to have a larder and utility rooms to hide things in.' The single-storey pen was built later than the barns. Its timber framework had disintegrated leaving an open shelter of hollow blockwork now rebuilt with the same materials and rendered white.

The dining room has a minimal, almost monastic quality suggested by the simple ash furniture and the commanding church tower silhouetted against the high, arched window

Although the front entrance is through the boarded barn doors, the most popular access is through the back door which leads into the kitchen and office wing. The kitchen has a minimal country style, pared of rustic clutter or pattern, with primrose walls, a terracotta floor and dado of white wooden cupboards. A scrubbed pine table, rush-seated chairs and dark-green Aga create an informal atmosphere, accentuated by a low, white ceiling. It contrasts with the lofty dining room next door that rises through the ground and first floors. Perhaps the presence of the church tower looming through the arched window intensifies the calm, almost monastic quality in the room. The sense of drama increases at night when the church is floodlit. 'You get the *lumière* without any *son*,' says Bob, 'especially in winter when the chestnut tree in front has no leaves.' Furniture is restricted to a long refectory table and simple dining chairs, both in ash to match the doors and floor. The only decoration is Alex's collection of antique glass displayed on open ash shelves. Beside the clear lead glass, lined like shadows on the cream wall, Victorian decanters and bowls throw sapphire and amethyst light into the room.

Double doors lead into a drawing room on two levels, which marks the join between the two barns. The dividing wall was knocked through, but the differing floor levels kept to vary the perspective and mood. The upper level, being less formal, is dominated by a small billiards table. The cobbled floor in the sheep pens was relaid on a terrace outside the drawing room. All the original openings have been converted into small-paned windows with deep ash sills that reveal the depth of the stone walls, insured against years of sheep occupation with dry lining laid behind plasterboard. Decoration follows Bob's preference for all things plain. Within a framework of white walls and oak ceiling joists, added colours are muted and neutral; oatmeal carpet, faded terracotta upholstery, linen curtains the colour of milky coffee hang from smooth gilt poles and geometric kilims that reflect each shade in the room. The simple white fireplace with an ash mantelpiece dotted with decoy ducks is flanked by a Chesterfield sofa and matching armchairs.

Instead of an outside ladder, the hayloft above is reached by stairs leading from the hall; it is an oblong space behind the dining room and lit by ventilation slits at ground and first-floor levels. After being unblocked these slits were widened slightly but left uncurtained for maximum light and simplicity. Upstairs, the arch of the barn door makes a stone curve against the white wall, adding a rough texture beside the smooth ash banisters. Three bedrooms and two bathrooms have been fitted into the first floor. The hayloft is the largest with a ceiling that follows the shape of the roof. Removing the ceiling joists and stud partition created extra volume and 'a slightly over-roomy atmosphere'. The trusses were then raised to support the roof, giving Bob and Alex a graphic pattern of diagonals to study from their large white bed. The three original openings and larger hayloft door are now windows, curtained with sprigged beige cotton. Groups of gilt-framed drawings and two reading lamps above the bed punctuate an expanse of white wall. Furniture is minimal; a Regency sofa upholstered with chocolate velvet in one corner; a deep blue armchair in another. There is a disciplined lack of clutter or clothes as everything is hidden from view in large, fitted cupboards and a dressing room-cum-bedroom next door.

Further up, tucked under the roof of the taller barn are two children's bedrooms and a bathroom over the dining room. Because of the roof's height, the tent-shaped rooms are of a generous size with little dormer windows fitted at floor and head height between a horizontal purlin. 'It was right at eye level,' explains Bob. 'Obviously you can't cut it, so the children have low windows to play by and a high dormer that brings light into the rooms.'

The garden has the same variety of levels as the interior. Transforming a 'crew' – Northamptonshire for bullock yard – from a mound of hardcore into a garden was a gruelling task. As the ground was uneven, Bob and Alex created a series of cobbled and flagstoned terraces and raised borders around a lawn. They imported 80 tons of topsoil by collecting residue filtered after washing sugar beet from a local factory. After six years the fine silky soil has encouraged a gentle English garden of herbaceous plants, shrubs and conifers. It has a secluded atmosphere sheltered by a barn and solid stone wall on two sides. A gate in the stone looks west across the flat water meadows of the River Nene – a flood plain that often overflows, freezing a winter skating rink across the fields.

MEADOW BARN
JOHN AND DIANA WORTHINGTON

~

The gracious proportions of the Worthingtons' library are more country house than barn. It is a long, low stately room lined with books on velvet clad shelves. Shuttered sash windows look out on to an English country garden of yew hedges, roses and lavender. But it *is* a barn, expertly tailored to the Worthingtons' requirements. Having decided to move from a large London house to the country, they needed enough space to contain their library. Diana Worthington had known for years that a barn, providing they could find one large enough, would be the answer.

Ten years ago there were no barns on the market. So while John, a don and historian, pursued his writing, Diana searched the Cotswolds for two years until she found a group of eighteenth-century farm buildings – two derelict barns and a farmhouse that had been empty for 15 years. Set in rural calm on the edge of a village, they were ideal for an extended family. There was one barn for the children and grandchildren, a larger barn for John and Diana, and a farmhouse which could be rented out. Each building needed complete renovation so by starting with the farmhouse the Worthingtons were able to live on site while the barns were restored.

The scale and shape of the large barn made a perfect framework for their plan. It is an L-shape with three gabled porches which, despite their original agricultural purpose, interrupt the stone walls and give a less barn-like appearance. The long side of the barn was 52 foot – a perfect library size – that dropped down into a manger to form the dining room and kitchen. A lower calf pen, at right angles to the barn was large enough for two bedrooms and bathrooms, with a

A prolific vine and bright clumps of achilleas shine against the Cotswold stone and muted grey woodwork

third attic-bedroom fitted above the manger.

As the Worthingtons knew precisely what they wanted, down to the smallest detail, they saw no point in using an architect. Instead they employed an efficient chartered surveyor and several talented local builders. Planning permission was given without any difficulty but as the barn was a listed building the Worthingtons were faced with two sets of criteria. Proposals for listed buildings did not necessarily match modern building regulations over light and air. 'It was not entirely unuseful to be able to balance one against the other,' says John. The windows caused a dispute between the two camps. 'The listing people didn't think sash windows were right for a barn. But we maintained that you must take every building on its own merit – and as the barn never had any windows to start with, how could they possibly tell?' Fortunately John and Diana's suggestion for small 'railway windows' – expanses of plain glass – was thwarted, as for practical reasons they would have been too small to meet building regulations for daylight.

The library forms the heart of the barn with its atmosphere of space and comfortable grandeur that percolates into the surrounding rooms. None has quite the same dimensions but each echoes the library's balance and generous proportions. 'I like space and serenity,' says Diana Worthington, explaining the stately four-foot doors that were widened further by the addition of moulded architraves. 'Too many doors look so mingy – as if a fat man has to go through sideways!' The narrowest entrance in the barn is a wicket door into the front hall. Inspired by one of their sons at Cambridge, it is set like a college gate into one side of the

boarded barn doors. (The prototype had to be expanded when their practical foreman observed it was not wide enough for a coffin to pass through.) A pair of tall, thin windows flank the barn doors adding light to the hall.

On arrival, the impression is of a modest baronial hall that reveals the barn's full height. A pale stone wall, the colour of shortbread, blends with the oak roof trusses and seagrass matting. Furniture stands out, old and robust; oak tables, chairs, chests, that contrast with a modern tapestry by Kaffe Fassett. The magnificence of the library is quite unexpected. Its air of permanence makes it hard to imagine its former life as a barn with a gaping roof. The Worthingtons knew that the right proportions were crucial to their design. Having lost six inches from the straightening of the uneven outer wall, they chose a ceiling height that exaggerated the width and gave balance to the room. From such a cavernous base they plotted where to put all the windows and doors. 'We had to improvise by standing on six-inch blocks over the mud floor and trying to visualize how it should be down to the last half inch,' explains John.

The interior has been designed by Diana, with the help of imaginative builders who made all the doors, windows, moulded cornices, the large stone fireplace and, most important of all, the bookcases. These had to be specially constructed to hold the deep shelves of irregular length that were bound in velvet to preserve the bindings of the books. Scumbled apricot walls give a warm, lived-in feeling, emphasized by the quantity of books around the room. But the symmetrical arrangement of fittings, furniture and ornaments lend a certain formality to the room; deep sofas at right angles to the fireplace leave space between for two Regency armchairs; sofa tables behind are laid with books, magazines, lamps and flowers.

The quantity of table lamps, nine in all, supplements the light from architectural tubes concealed above the bookcases. Heating is equally discreet. Radiators are hidden behind painted grilles beneath the window seats and behind bookcases where an asbestos lining below the shelves protects the books from the heat. Against the apricot walls and fawn carpets, added colour is calm and neutral, echoing the stone fireplace

To contrast with the rest of the interior, the entrance hall retains the uninterrupted barn height, revealing a high pitched roof striped with oak rafters and beams

and off-white woodwork. Furnishings have simple pattern and texture; mustard-cotton ticking on one sofa, a straw-yellow diamond weave on the other; curtains in cream sailcloth edged with knotted webbing. A surprising homespun touch is the curtain rod made from a young tree trunk. It was bought as a present from Diana for John's study but it actually fitted the largest of the library windows, where it now hangs like a rustic lintel over a gap left by the derelict barn doors.

Diana and John both have a study in the square porches at the back of the barn. They jut out, companionably, into the garden giving much needed shelter and extra walls for roses to climb. Originally both rooms had barn doors where there are now windows. (The only remaining doors in the barn were a pair hanging from their hinges in John's study which were moved across the hall to the front entrance.) Both studies open off the library through glass-paned doors; personal sanctums where John writes and researches history, engulfed by more books, piled on his desk and lining the walls, whilst Diana's study is pale and pretty with apricot walls and tea-coloured cotton moiré curtains. All the wall colours were mixed by Diana from her artists' oil paints. She then took her jam jars to a paint expert in Chelsea, London, who reproduced the colours in larger quantities. The burnt apricot for the library came from scumbling glaze over a base of bright pink emulsion.

Her intended colour scheme for the dining room and kitchen was a pale lettuce green. The result, more a greeny cream, can be glimpsed from the library through a mahogany and glass door. It opens on to wide stone steps that lead down to the manger that was rebuilt to form a semi-open-plan dining room and kitchen with low beamed ceilings. The most striking feature in the dining room is its dark-green table and chairs. As the room was to have a light, rather Italian feel, the Worthingtons decided their traditional furniture would look out of place. Inspired by a table from Ragley Hall in Warwickshire they drew a splayed-leg oval design for their builders who reproduced an exact copy two weeks later – just in time for Christmas. Diana painted the table legs and cane seated chairs in pine green, then stippled the chipboard table top, defining

the edges with a darker band of colour. Matching tapestry cushions, patterned with cabbages and cauliflowers, sit on each chair, five sewn by Diana, the others by two kind friends.

The symmetry of the library reappears in the dining room. Two deep rectangular alcoves lined with blue and white china flank the doorway above Regency side tables. An upright piano stands between two grey scagliola marble columns that were made years ago to hold cut-glass candle lamps. The floor, emphasizing the continental atmosphere, is laid with small French clay tiles which range in colour from terracotta to pale honey. They extend into the kitchen which is separated from the dining room by a partition wall. Because all the everyday essentials are kept in a larder and utility room, converted from an outbuilding beyond, the kitchen is remarkably cool and un-cluttered. Its simplicity recalls an old-fashioned dairy with cream cupboards against buttermilk walls, white tiles and a deep, shuttered window. Instead of curtains the eye is caught by a garniture of earthenware across the sill.

A door between the kitchen and dining room leads into a sheltered corner of the garden. It has taken ten years of careful nurturing to turn what was a patch of windswept farmland into a classic country garden. As there were no trees it needed some form and shelter from persistent winds. Anything too orna-mental would have looked out of place beside the landscape of grazing cows, so the Worthingtons planted willows, an orchard and a wild flower meadow scattered with moon daisies and cowslips. Closer to the barn a stone wall extending from Diana's study divides the garden into two compartments. Her window overlooks a terrace edged in clumps of lavender, alche-milla and roses, which steps down to a lawn bordered by herba-ceous plants. In summer, below the library windows, Regale lilies grow in terracotta pots encircled by cushions of thyme. A yellow tree-peony flourishes in the crook of the wall, under-planted with sedum and marjoram. Yew hedges are being grown as windbreaks, one beneath a row of bleached horn-beams. Yet they do not enclose the entire garden. Through a wide gap, a long view connects the barn with the landscape.

The elegant and generous proportions of the library establish the settled atmosphere of an English country house

THE HOP KILNS
PAUL CHANDLER AND URSULA MASON

—— ~ ——

The hop kilns loom from the Worcestershire skyline like an agricultural fortress. The red brick towers with conical grey roofs and white cowls are not an unusual landmark, for this is hop country. But in Worcestershire, a building with six round kilns is unique. Paul Chandler and Ursula Mason live and work in this mid-Victorian giant that was in use as the co-operative hop kiln until the early 1960s. They discovered it during the parched summer of 1976. Like an oasis in a desert, it was surrounded by a brilliant greenness of hops and fruit trees. Ursula fell in love at first sight. As it suited all their criteria of somewhere to live with sufficient space to run a business in a beautiful part of the country, they bought it.

The top floor of the hop kilns had been partly converted for domestic use and was just habitable from the start. With such acres of space Paul and Ursula were able to camp *in situ* while contemplating their new living and business quarters. The rest of the three-storey building had been virtually untouched. It consisted of a central area of 60 by 40 feet on each floor, surrounded by six kilns containing circular soaring rooms at ground and top level.

Beneath the dirt and pungent debris, the hop kilns might easily have roared back into action. After the September harvest the hops would have been processed through the winter, laid on slatted floors in the middle of the kilns, then tossed and dried by fires in the ground chambers. Once dried they were tipped down chutes into the first floor central area, then compressed and bagged up into long sacks.

But instead of brewing, the ground and first floors were an obvious base for an embryonic ceramic business. After an advertising career in London, Ursula went to Stoke to learn the workings of the pottery industry, following her husband's theory that practical know-how plus marketing skills and a sound design input equals a viable business. So, combining her acquired knowledge with Paul's screen printing expertise, they started a company producing decorated plant pots and holders.

The hop kilns loom like an agricultural giant on the Worcestershire skyline – a towering legacy of the late nineteenth century when a quarter of the English hop harvest came from this area

47

Five years later they expanded into the gift business, selling decorative tin ware and kitchen ceramics – these were produced in the ground floor pottery, then fired in kilns within the old hop kilns.

Creating a home out of the top floor was not such a smooth transition. Leading off the central living area with its double-pitched wooden roof were six round rooms with walls one brick deep, three small windows and 30-foot conical ceilings. (Round hop kilns were built in Worcestershire from 1835 as they were more economical structures and produced a better draught.) To live in they were cold and rather dark with awkward proportions. The first priority was to convert one of the kilns into a bedroom. Ursula, rather like Goldilocks in a strange house, tackled one bedroom, found it too cold and moved on to another. Lowering the pointed ceiling to encourage warmth and cosiness had no effect on the temperature in the first kiln and during their first winter Ursula caught pneumonia. This first round yellow room has become Paul's study. Having left Ursula to run the ceramics business, he is now involved in computer software and politics, standing as the Liberal Democrat candidate for South Worcestershire.

Paul and Ursula sleep in the adjacent kiln where the walls were insulated, then covered with plasterboard before any dec-

Paul and Ursula sleep in a split-level kiln, encircled by a mural of the Shropshire and Worcestershire countryside; a romantic landscape that stretches the 25-foot span from floor to roof

oration began. They made full use of the height by dividing it between a split level sleeping gallery, bathroom and dressing room. The tower-like proportions suggest a fairytale setting accentuated by a mural, painted from floor to pinnacle, of a romantic landscape seen through the bars of a birdcage. The artist, Priscilla Kennedy, combined the surrounding Shropshire and Worcestershire countryside with fictional landmarks, re-siting Daphne du Maurier's Manderley in the Malvern Hills.

The bed, set almost in the painted clouds, is reached by a steep staircase around the wall leading up to a balconied gallery. Below, there is a curved dressing room and bathroom, painted with a connecting trellis of honeysuckle and wisteria. The split-level scheme has been repeated across the building in their small son Quentin's kiln, giving him a nursery at ground level with a curved staircase up to bed. At eye level his walls are painted with nursery rhyme characters, while higher up, rockets and spaceships soar against a dark night sky.

Ursula soon realized that round rooms are not practical or easy to furnish. 'It does mean you need less furniture, as it all looks so prominent,' she says. 'You can't push anything into a corner.' As each kiln was converted, the dwindling storage space became a problem – ironic in such a huge area. The only practical solution was to build a walk-in larder and store room in a corner of the living room. In spite of draughtiness and mammoth proportions, and the comparative cosiness of other rooms, it is conscientiously kept as the sitting room. 'I do long for cosiness, especially from October to April,' Ursula says. 'It's relaxing in front of the television when you feel it most.' But though perhaps without achieving snugness, the central area, carpeted and warmed by a Jotul wood stove, has a comfortable air. There are sofas, armchairs, floor cushions, table lamps and plants. Free additional heat from kiln firings in the pottery rises through open trap doors. Blackened oak posts and trusses were not scorched by inner heat but by an incendiary bomb dropped on the building in the war. As so much of the wall space is taken up by six double doors into the kilns, the only natural light comes through a dormer in the roof and a row of small uncurtained windows around the wall. As a back up, there are table lamps and spotlights angled from the beams.

While concentrating on the bedrooms, Paul and Ursula made do with the kitchen and bathroom adapted by the previous owners. Both kilns had been truncated, lopping off the cowl top and pointed roof to a nine-foot ceiling. But, as it had been a shoestring process, the thin walls had begun to rot and sprout mushrooms. After seven years, when their business was thriving, they felt they could afford to raze both rooms to floor level and rebuild them more substantially. The operation cost twice the price of the hop kilns and the surrounding half acre. 'There is nothing cheap about this place,' insists Ursula. 'Putting our expenses against the business is the only way we can afford it.'

Re-using the original bricks, the kilns grew back into shorter conical towers with tiled roofs that match the central building.

Instead of the cream rendering on the four original kilns, the new towers have a semi-circle of windows that fill the kitchens and bathroom with panoramic views of Worcestershire. From the airy tiled bathroom you can see the hop kilns' successor across the fields – a more mundane red-brick construction that reflects the mechanization of the industry today. A century ago there would have been hundreds of workers in the fields, handpicking each hop flower from its stalk.

The kitchen is a light, sunny room where function and comfort work together. It has a modern high-tech speckled grey-and-white colour scheme that contrasts with the agricultural outlook. Fitted kitchen units line the curved walls, above and below a tiled work surface with an in-built hob and comforting white Aga. The practical elements are diluted by colourful modern prints, plants, books and Quentin's toys. A glass door opens on to a balcony which can also be reached through French windows in Paul and Ursula's bedroom. Here, there is just enough space for a table and potted herbs, making an al fresco dining room and miniature garden in summer. Plans for an external staircase to the garden below have been postponed because of its exorbitant cost, so that at present the only way out is down through the office floor and pottery. 'Regardless of all this space, it is like living in a flat,' says Ursula. 'I love being in the garden, but it is rather an expedition to get down there, especially with a small child.' When there is time she goes down in the evening to tend an orderly vegetable patch. The surrounding wasteland is now a garden where, beyond a courtyard, shrubs and fruit trees grow. Dark-green ivy creeping up one kiln seems an appropriate bridge between man and the Worcestershire landscape.

COLLOPS BARN
ALAN AND JILL WYATT

~

Essex is a county where agriculture has outgrown traditional farm buildings. An increasing number stand rejected along the skyline of the flat open landscape – long, threshing barns clad in blackened elm with slate or peg-tiled roofs. Collops Barn is a classic example, set around a courtyard with a cowshed, outbuildings and granary. It was a working farm until five years ago when the scale of modern machinery outgrew the barns' dimensions. Manoeuvring tractors between eighteenth-century cart doors became impossible. The only solution was to sell up and move on. The farmer offered his buildings to Alan and Jill Wyatt who lived in a farmhouse behind the courtyard. Neither was a farmer; Alan was a lawyer, Jill a teacher, but they couldn't resist the farmer's offer. Then for three years the buildings stood empty, costing the Wyatts a fortune in basic maintenance. 'It became ridiculous, especially after the hurricane in 1987. We were just spending and spending endlessly,' recalls Jill. So rather than paying out to prop the buildings up they decided to go ahead and live in them.

The conversion was planned with meticulous respect for the original structure and appearance of the barns and outbuildings and, being a Grade Two listed building, planning permission was granted at the first request. The result, though a spectacular home, 'is still very much a pair of barns,' Alan says, 'and, if necessary, the internal walls could come out and the barns taken back into agricultural use.' The courtyard's character comes from the different age, shape and materials of the buildings. The two threshing barns, containing the house, are eighteenth century; the lower one built fifty years before its neighbour. Their long boarded façade is fronted by a slate-roofed open cowhouse added in the eighteenth century, and now a glass walled kitchen. A cowshed of the same period stands at right angles to the barns, clad in similar elm boarding with a tiled roof. It has been converted into an office for Alan's law practice and headquarters for the Wyatts' ski-travel company, Over the Hill, that specializes in holidays for the over-forties. The conversion was an ambitious undertaking, structu-

The blackened elm cladding and unbroken tiled roof keep the appearance of a traditional Essex barn, domesticated by glazed cart doors and gables

rally and financially. As both barns had to be rebuilt from foundations to roof, it was like creating a new house within the confines of an uncompromising framework. The only cheap commodity was an inherent supply of character.

The Wyatts were blessed with an expert builder who understood the need for traditional methods and materials. Despite the amount of work involved, it took only one intensive year to complete and involved employing as many as 14 men at times. The Wyatts were involved in every stage and, as they lived and worked next door, could be on site at any time to supervise setbacks or deviations from the architect's plans. As Jill explains with some understatement, 'It wasn't just a case of cleaning up.' The whole building had to be stripped down to a framework of open timbers, then rewalled, reroofed and, in the case of the older barn, underpinned. Old cement cleared from the base of the walls revealed crumbling beams so proper foundations had to be dug out and a new base plate installed below a red-brick plinth. Above, the walls were reclad with traditional creosoted elm boarding, a pliable wood that twists and bends with age, giving Essex barns their weathered, slightly haphazard outline. In keeping with that tradition, the roof of Collops Barn has been retiled following the undulating dips and curves of the original. The old peg-tiles were salvaged and relaid at the back of the barn but similar ones had to be found for the front, to replace the corrugated tin and asbestos that had been used to patch the roof.

The living space is cleverly organized to avoid any obvious demarcation between the barns. In the lower barn a stepped entrance hall rises into an enormous sitting room which leads to a dining hall, bedrooms and bathroom in the adjoining building. Originally both barns were open from floor to roof with a pair of traditional high cart doors on opposing walls. The full height has been retained in parts of both barns which gives an impression of minimal change and lends full impact to the network of beams that dominate every view. As there was not enough height for two storeys in the lower barn, it was kept open from ground to rafters. Such a towering space made a dramatic entrance hall but felt too cavernous for a sitting

A graphic pattern of diagonal timbers and herringboned bricks dominate the dining hall which fills the two storey height

room. A compromise was reached whereby the sitting room floor was raised two feet above ground level, providing more livable dimensions without loss of airiness. It was Jill's idea to use the dead space below for a cellar. 'I asked the builders to give me a hole in the ground that I could stand in and use for storage.' It also houses the controls for an under-floor central heating system, Flo Rad, a zoned network of water heated pipes that operate at a lower temperature than conventional systems. All the practical aspects of the barn have been carefully planned. No wires, radiators or flexes are visible. Discreet spotlights and downlighters are tucked between the roof trusses. Speakers wired to a remote control hi-fi system are slotted into wall vents throughout the barns. 'One of the joys of starting from scratch is that you can have exactly what you want, where you want – and all the wiring can be hidden away,' says Jill.

Both sets of main doors have been glazed so light floods in from either side. Triangular windows fitted between the gable above let in further light. The larger windows are fitted with Capa Float glass which regulates the inside temperature, avoiding a greenhouse effect from strong sunlight. Upstairs, windows have been added only where essential and, because they had to be fitted around the beams, are smaller and higher than ideal. Two red-brick chimney were added at each end of the barns; one for the fireplace, one for the boiler. 'We were lucky that the Essex planners allowed an external brick chimney. As an industrial type of building, they recommend that a barn should keep its industrial flue pipe.' Happily, the brick passed scrutiny and the fireplace could take centre stage in the sitting room. It was constructed around a massive oak bressumer – a traditional fireplace beam moulded with age into a camphored shape that encourages a fire's draught. Following a regional pattern, the red bricks were cut down to Tudor size, then stepped up into a hip-shaped fire surround above the beam.

Having raised the level of the sitting room, its original brick threshing floor was taken up, turned over and relaid in the dining hall. The honey-coloured herringbone design makes a rustic background to the oak posts that stripe the walls in a graphic pattern. The dining hall, which spans the barn's full height, is given added interest by an oak staircase to a galleried landing panelled with bookshelves. The master bedroom and en-suite bathroom, which lead off the landing, have been juggled ingeniously around a tie beam sandwiched in the middle of a wall. The only possible route from bedroom to bathroom was to cut a high trap door between the beams putting stairs on either side, like a step ladder. Once inside, the bathroom feels like a pretty wooden cabin lined with cream-painted panelling. Decoration on both levels keeps to soft neutral colours. Except for the brick-floored dining hall, the oatmeal carpets throughout tone with the cream walls and various shades of oak that fill every room. Furniture is also in oak-country antiques that have moved from farmhouse to barn.

Everything is neutral until you move from the dining hall into the old bull pen. Rechristened the 'Spa', it is a startling contrast to the rest of the barn with its smooth white walls, scarlet ceramic floor and round Jacuzzi edged with black and

Steps on either side of the beams provide the only logical route between the master bedroom and bathroom. Once inside it is decorated like a cosy wooden cabin with cream panelled walls.

white mosaic tiles. These bold colours continue along a passage of utility rooms converted from the adjoining outbuildings. A back door opens into a garden behind the barn where a tennis court has been levelled out of a two-acre field.

The kitchen combines high-tech gadgetry with the pale colours of the barn interior. It is a long, gleaming room, lit by a south-facing wall of glass which gives an all-seeing view around the courtyard. To temper the sunlight, Jill has chosen ice-blue colours; white walls, pale blue ceramic floor tiles with cupboards and shelves sponged and dragged blue over white that fit just below the beams. The layout is precision planned but obviously user-friendly. Even the triple sinks on a central unit face outward so there is no feeling of being left out behind the scenes peeling potatoes. Emphasized by the expanse of glass and sunlight, the kitchen has a fresh, continental atmosphere that contrasts with the rustic spirit in the rest of the barn. Spend too long basking in the warmth and the Essex countryside could seem to retreat. Yet it is always there, a pattern of fields stretching for miles under changing skies.

THE COWSHED

KEN MELLOR

—— ~ ——

The cows were still in residence when Ken Mellor discovered his Cotswold retreat 14 years ago. They lived on the cobbled ground floor, munching fodder from the store above. It is unlikely that they appreciated their location, but to Ken it was irresistible. The Windrush Valley had always been one of his favourite haunts – and here he discovered a modest stone cowshed on the river bank that had the makings of a dream house. It belonged to a local farmer whose buildings dominated the tiny hamlet of Windrush. He had not thought of selling but names and addresses were exchanged just in case. Six months later Ken returned to an empty shed. The farmer was more friendly but still non-committal. As the old roof needed repair he was building a better home for his cows. After much deliberation and against his wife's wishes, he agreed to sell. Ken had a financial limit that did not stretch to the £15,000 price suggested by the farmer's agent. Both sides agreed to compromise at £12,500. 'It seemed a lot at the time for a ruin that needed much more money spent on it to make it into a house.'

Apart from its thick stone walls and Cotswold slate roof in dubious order, the Victorian building had little to boast about. The only access between the ground and boarded floor above was a slot for pushing fodder down to the cows. There was a door and external staircase on the roadside and another door and three poky openings on the riverside. As the charm of the place was its river-bank site and views across the valley, it made sense to open out that aspect. The result is a virtual wall of glass overlooking the Windrush river and valley beyond. The

landscape was dominated, 14 years ago, by giant elm trees, but because of the ravages of Dutch Elm disease they had to be felled. The gap they left behind is now filled by a large man-made lake dug out by the farmer to attract water birds and wildlife. It acts like a gigantic mirror, magnifying the light in the valley and creating curious optical illusions on windy days when the river races past the slow moving lake.

As the building was an empty shell, Ken had the freedom to start from scratch. He is an architect who trained and practised in Yorkshire before working in London for the now disbanded Greater London Council. After that he gravitated to theatre and television set design. But staging his own home was a dilemma. 'I was doubtful in my own mind exactly what I should do or what the local planners would allow,' explains Ken. He had renovated town houses but this was his first country conversion. Fortunately he was helped by an enlightened planning authority architect, who gave him unexpected freedom to produce what he wanted.

There was no urgency. Ken gave himself six months to potter with plans and drawings; experimenting with the layout of the kitchen, dining room, bedrooms and bathrooms. His first idea was to contain everything within the original walls but, as the setting was so idyllic, he decided to extend the buildings by the addition of a square stone tower that juts out at right angles to the cowshed. It looks quite in keeping yet adds a delightful eccentricity to the place; a squat Cotswold folly topped with an antique weather-vane. Beneath the stone pyramid roof is Ken's studio with its oblong windows

The restored cowshed with far-reaching views over land and water nestles beside Ken Mellor's addition of a Cotswold tower with a pyramid roof

wrapping three sides of the room. Underneath, there is space for a bedroom with a high arched window and Ken's marble and mirror bathroom.

The tower and cowshed are linked by the blue and white tiled kitchen, fronted by a glass wall that slides open into the garden. The extra space in the tower gave more scope to the cowshed design. To capitalize on the view, Ken put the sitting room upstairs in the old fodder store; a long, open ended space curtailed by a balcony overlooking the dining room. The greatest impact in the sitting room is the wall-sized window that opens on to a narrow wooden terrace, rather like the deck of a ship. Its 20 foot length meant that Ken had to wait six months for the double glazed sheet of glass to arrive. Disaster seemed almost inevitable. It struck while the floor was being sanded. 'The machine took off from the middle of the floor like a robot and ploughed straight through the new window,' recalls Ken, amused only in retrospect.

A stone spiral staircase built into a projecting bay window on the roadside leads down to the dining room. With its marble floors and octagonal stone column there is a sense of Cotswold cowshed meeting Roman villa. 'Early visits to Italy certainly had an effect on my design,' explains Ken. He had envisaged stone floors to match the staircase but old Cotswold stone was in short supply and new stone cost more than the

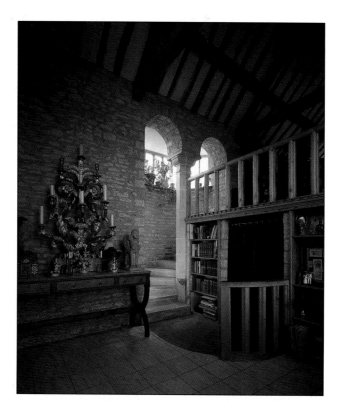

ABOVE, *Ken's sense of drama is obvious in the dining hall where the marble floor, arched stairwell and ornate candelabra establish a theatrical atmosphere*

RIGHT, *Against rough stone walls and a lofty pitched roof, the sitting room exudes an air of robust comfort*

end of line marble found from a source in Vauxhall. On first impression, the dining room spans the full height of the building, but with a small floor space Ken found the double height too oppressive and tower-like. To balance the proportions, the floor was raised to a slightly mezzanine level, built up by steps from the entrance lobby.

One of the drawbacks to the cowshed was its orientation. The riverside, facing northwest, was deprived of morning sunlight. Instead of extra windows looking south on to the road, Ken installed protruding glass lantern lights in the kitchen and bathroom roofs, which were lined with mirrored glass for extra brightness. The square openings make useful places for hanging plants whose leaves add a greenish glow to the reflected light. Finances were a crucial factor throughout the conversion. Ken was lucky to find a talented local builder but, as workmen were paid on a daily rate rather than a fixed contract, he had no concept of the final cost. As the money supply dwindled he was forced to compromise on quality and use cheaper deal instead of oak for the interior and external woodwork. The floors have survived well, but using cheap softwood outside was a false economy, much regretted by Ken. 'It is far less resistant which means spending more now on maintenance and repainting.'

Inside there is no hint of austerity. Oil fired central heating

shields the cowshed from the Cotswold east winds and is boosted by a woodburning stove in the sitting room. 'I wanted an open fireplace but thought how could I possibly do another Cotswold reproduction in this area?' Ken had admired a cast-iron Franklin stove in America and tracked down the first one imported to England. Its uninsulated chimney flue stretching from stove to pitched roof acts as an enormous tubular radiator.

Ken's decoration is robust with flamboyant touches. Against the rough stone walls, substantial armchairs, a *chaise-longue* and Knole sofa upholstered in an oatmeal herringbone furnish the room with relaxed comfort, over which towers an umbrella of giant hogweed. The dining room has a theatrical eccentricity, exaggerated by an ornate Baroque candelabra and the unlikely presence of a stag's head – trophies inherited from a stage set. Oak shelving from an old nunnery via a local antique shop, has been adapted and made into a bookcase across one wall, topped with a carved wooden cornice.

The cowshed may not be in true Cotswold style but shows a strong allegiance to local tradition. Whenever possible original materials were recycled. Old Cotswold stone was used on the tower and local Stonesfield slates on the roof. These were laid to match the cowshed roof with small pieces of slate at the ridge and larger pieces at the eaves. Weather-boarding on the studio tower is painted in an authentic Cotswold olive-drab. The terraced garden is paved with cobbled stones dug from the cowshed floor. Larger stones from the old workhouse at Witney were turned into steps that lead to the sitting room balcony. The garden has been cultivated from a sloping river bank into an informal group of terraces, divided by a central flight of stone steps. It is planted with low-maintenance shrubs that thrive in the boggy conditions – cornus, hebes, mahonias, hellebores, yellow irises, daffodils. 'I didn't want the garden to look too careful. It had to grow into the land,' explains Ken. Well-weathered furniture is positioned at strategic points to watch the swans and occasional kingfisher dart by. On sunny days the most inviting place is a terrace at the water's edge, shaded by a canopy of honeysuckle and buddleia.

WALLS END

ANTONIA AND CHRISTOPHER THYNNE

~

In summer Antonia and Christopher Thynne take weekends in the middle of the week. It is the only time that Christopher can escape from Longleat in Wiltshire where he runs the ancestral home and safari park. Fortunately, their bolt hole is conveniently close – just 90 minutes from Longleat in the Cotswold village of Quennington.

It is called Walls End. Not, as friends presume, after Antonia's other family home near Newcastle, but after its last occupant, Mr Wall. He was the gardener for the large house next door where Antonia spent her childhood. Originally it was a small cow byre, built in the late eighteenth century, where the Rector kept two or three cows below a hayloft. There were no cows in Mr Wall's day and the dark cobbled byre had become a woodstore with a saddle room at one end where the groom would gut rabbits. Next door was an apple store, beyond that, Mr Wall's privy.

Antonia was given the derelict building by her mother five years ago. It was in a shambolic state but the setting beside the River Coln, hidden from view by an overgrown kitchen garden, was perfect. The conversion to a Cotswold cottage was designed by the architect Nicky Johnston. Although not quite on his usual scale, he took it on as a friend. 'We felt rather cheeky asking him to do anything so paltry,' says Antonia. 'It must have made quite a contrast to Paul Getty's castle in Buckinghamshire!'

What is so ingenious about his design is the amount that has been fitted into such a small, cottage space. The ground floor is divided between two rooms; a surprisingly long low drawing room,

A smooth lawn has replaced the overgrown kitchen garden in front of Walls End. Fifty years ago it housed a woodstore, saddle room, apple store and Mr Wall, the gardener's, privy.

which was originally the cow byre, and the kitchen which had been the apple store and gardener's privy. 'We wanted to have one room far larger than you think the house could take,' says Christopher. 'After all, if you sit in one big room, it doesn't matter how small the rest are.' There was space in the loft above the cow byre for two bedrooms and tiny bathrooms. As the apple store was a single storey building the Thynnes decided to expand upward and outward to make a third bedroom with space below for a narrow hall, cloakroom and utility room, 'How I *hate* that word,' exclaims Christopher.

They wanted the addition to merge with the original building which meant finding some old Cotswold stone. Antonia had noticed a crumbling barn on an eccentric uncle's estate close by at Hatherop and wrote to ask if she could buy it. A reply came back from her uncle's agent 'that Sir Thomas would like a gift element in the sale,' and suggested the precise sum of £228.10. So for the convenience of having his barn removed, Christopher and Antonia acquired a valuable quantity of stone, tile and cobbles – more than enough for their new walls, roof, stone garage (that looks like a tiny Cotswold barn), and repairs to the existing structure.

The conversion took an unhurried two years and was carried out in bursts when the builder, another friend called Hal Wynne-Jones, had time to spare. The place had to be gutted; the cobbled floor lifted and moved outside, a damp course, heating, plumbing and wiring installed. A curious event was the discovery of a cat that had been bricked into a little hollow in the wall – a relic of previous

builders' superstitions or a touch of local witchcraft? 'Whatever it was, nobody except us seemed too surprised at finding a cat in the wall,' recalls Christopher.

As the byre was pitch black the ground level openings were unboarded and made into small-paned cottage windows – painted white below wooden lintels. The original entrance was kept, but replaced by a wide glass door with panes that matched the windows. The loft, reached by a staircase from the saddle room, was lit by one dormer window in the middle of the roof. It has been exchanged for two gabled dormers, faced with stone tiles that perch right on the eaves above the ground-floor windows. Whilst the old byre has a traditional stone front, the extension and apple store are boarded with wooden planks similar to the original building. Except for a tall stone roof, it has a look that remains part potting shed, part summer-house. A large bay window – added to increase the kitchen space – interrupts the wooden façade which Christopher plans to cover with climbing plants.

The interior has a relaxed indulgent atmosphere. 'We come here to do absolutely nothing,' says Antonia. It may be a week-end retreat but it is very much a home, decorated and fur-nished with attention to comfort. There are few concessions to the cottage proportions. The drawing room is filled in country-house scale with large sofas, armchairs, draped tables, lamps and a *chaise-longue*. Somehow there is no overcrowding – the room would probably look empty without its quota of chairs and small tables. Its fullness and mix of pattern recall a Victorian drawing room, without the gloom. The pistachio-green of the walls is echoed by the opulent chintz curtains, scattered with coral lilies, that hang below ornate pelmets groaning with zigzagged and frilled borders. There is an abun-dance of cushions, some flowery, others plain and silky, banked-up like sugared almonds across a sofa.

A white marble fireplace from Longleat, 'slightly over-grand for this house,' dominates one end of the room. It is one of a

The sitting room, 'far larger than you think the cottage could take,' has a relaxed indulgent mood. Much of the furniture is borrowed from Antonia Thynne's antique shop in the stable yard at Longleat.

pair that had been relegated to the cellar, so Christopher's father, the Marquis of Bath, passed it on to him. Much of the furniture and ornaments come from Longleat; not from the family home, but from Antonia's antiques shop in the stable yard which was denuded of tables, chairs, mirrors and candlesticks to fill Walls End. Other pieces come from previous homes. Some are Christopher's bargains tracked down in the early 1960s or before. The brass fender around the fireplace was found, coated with filth and white paint, in a London junk shop for 27s 6d. 'It was a bargain even in those days – but what I *really* wanted to find was a Rubens, not a fender.' Its seat is upholstered in a coral and beige bargello pattern, matching a sofa and mahogany *chaise-longue* – colours that blend with the seagrass matting on the floor and stairs.

The staircase, slightly altered from its previous position, leads from a corner of the drawing room. Beside the stairs hang a set of Arcimboldo's fantasy helmets; photographs of the originals printed in black and gold on to glass. They were another bargain, bought 30 years ago from the impoverished printer for £12. A large gilt mirror borrowed from Antonia's shop hangs on the wall at right angles to the photographs, reflecting them from different angles. It also catches a group of moulded clay plaques hung over the stairs, adding a valuable illusion of space to the staircase and landing.

Christopher and Antonia's bedroom is just large enough for 'the folly', a regal mahogany four-poster squeezed into place. Apart from its age and Sheraton pedigree the bed has great sentimental value. It is an old family piece that was lost for seven years in the South of France. Once found and shipped home, Christopher and Antonia simply had to use it. 'I rather love the folly of having a bed much too big for the room – but it cost us a fortune in building,' says Christopher. As the entrance was too narrow, the bed had to come up through the floorboards in pieces. Then as the bed was too tall, the ceiling had to be raised.

It could be an important marital issue. 'Basically everything including the house belongs to Antonia, except the bed,' explains Christopher. 'If I ever think of leaving her, I'd have to decide whether I wanted to stay and keep the bed, or leave her and lose the bed.' It is elaborately draped with frilled chintz hangings and a tasselled canopy lined in carnation pink. The same Jane Churchill green, pink and blue flowered chintz hangs at the dormer window; the fabric is slotted on to towel rails that swing right back against the wall to give maximum daylight.

There is just space to open a door into a tiny ensuite bathroom which looks out to Quennington church – renowned for its exquisite Norman carvings around the doors. In the upstairs arrangement the only sacrifice made was over storage space. An extra bathroom took priority over cupboards. The spare room overlooking the garden and river is decorated with green geometric wallpaper from Osborne and Little. This room shares the second bathroom with Sophie Thynne's more spacious bedroom between the eaves. Its sloping attic proportions are accentuated by simple blue and white furnishings against a seagrass matting floor. A white iron bedstead stands under a window, flanked by low white chests for books and column lamps.

As there was no space for a dining room, meals are eaten in the kitchen. A table and semi-circle of old church pews fill the curve of a deep bay window, away from the practical side of the kitchen. Not that it is intended for elaborate cooking, 'Although people do come and stay sometimes in the winter when we have proper weekends,' says Antonia. The pale apricot walls are lined with pine cupboards, fitted between a cooker, fridge and double-sink. But the bay window is the focus of the room, giving it a light, sunny atmosphere. The cushioned pews, bought from an architectural salvage source in Cirencester, make an inviting place to count ducks as they glide past the edge of the garden.

The four poster folly was squeezed through the floorboards into Christopher and Antonia's bedroom. After raising the roof, it rests in regal splendour, leaving just enough space for bedside tables.

WATERGATE FARM

SUE AND GEOFFREY SMART

~

Large farmhouses seldom come on to the market in Northumberland, particularly in the Tyne Valley beside Hadrian's Wall. Here narrow lanes meander off the straight Roman Road and run along a rolling patchwork of stone walled fields speckled with buttercups. In such countryside a new house stands out like an unwelcome intruder, but the Smarts' converted farmbuildings, on the edge of the village of Great Whittington, have roots in the eighteenth century. Geoffrey Smart, too, belongs to this land. His parents, who now live across the fields, used to farm the surrounding land and Geoffrey remembers how, as a child, he helped to whitewash the buildings' grey stone walls – walls that have now become part of his drawing room.

Originally the structure was L-shaped with a barn along one side and a two-storey granary at right angles. As the farm tractors outgrew the wagon doors and the barn had to be mucked out by hand, the buildings became impractical and neglected. Geoffrey and his wife Sue realized the potential for a house and began an extraordinary transformation in 1983. The architect stayed one week, then left after a disagreement over the design. 'He wanted the buildings to look like a conversion, we wanted them to look like a house,' explains Sue. As the Smarts were living on site in a farm cottage they decided to organize the whole process themselves; its design, structure, fittings and eventually the decoration.

The plan was brave. Stripped of its lean-to Dutch barn at the back and tin porch at the front, the sandstone base of the building needed expanding. Instead of spreading outwards, the Smarts went upwards, lifting the slate roof to create a second storey that doubled the height of the building. 'I was scared stiff it might not blend in and the whole thing would look like a sandwich,' recalls Geoffrey. But the extension is an almost identical match, built in sandstone from a demolished stable block at nearby Arcot Hall. Geoffrey bought the whole building, extracting a front door lintel, massive quoins for the wall corners and replacement roofing slates.

With hindsight Geoffrey and Sue regret keeping the barn's original 15-foot width. 'It would have been three days' extra work to make it wider. The walls were already halfway down and it would have cost very little extra, but you count every penny at that stage,' says Geoffrey. There is no feeling of pinched pennies or space in the rambling five-bedroomed house. What stands out is the meticulous attention given to detail throughout the house; the importance attached to the right windows, doors, mouldings, fireplaces, bathroom fittings. As the house grew, Sue became engrossed in one phase after another. 'You tend to get stuck on one thing. I had to rush round and look at everyone's lintels, then skirting boards, then light fittings. It sounds stupid, but when you put all the details together you realize how important they are.'

The Smarts were amazed at how fast the building progressed until they realized that the structure alone counted for about a quarter of the overall cost. The interior fittings and decoration were far more expensive and time consuming than they had envisaged. They had begun with an empty structure which had one internal wall between the barn and granary. The spaces either side were open to the roof, furnished with relics of past occupants: a stone trough in the barn where cows had fed; an antique corn crusher that ground the grain pitched through a hole above.

Before the Smarts' conversion, the sandstone barn and granary formed a long low L-shape, fronted by a lean-to Dutch barn

Although the building has changed almost beyond recognition, six original doors remain. Apart from the front door, they are all glazed which gives a light sunny feeling and a strong link to the surrounding garden. Inside and out, there is an intentional Georgian character, emphasized by traditional sash windows and smooth stone lintels. 'Our idea was not to make it feel like a new house but at the same time not to feel like a false old house,' says Sue. Instead of keeping the irregular

The barn and granary, expanded by a barely detectable second storey – Geoffrey's worries that it would look like a sandwich did not come true

levels, the Smarts built up the lower end to make an even ground floor. The kitchen however is raised to give a wider outlook over the fields and avoid eye contact with tractors on the farm lane outside the window.

The rooms are laid out in a conventional pattern that unites the granary and barn. The granary is divided between a small sitting room and a farmhouse kitchen above which are a guest room and attic playroom. The far end of the granary stood lower than the rest of the building, but by lifting the roof and adding three foot to the walls, a generous attic room was created, lit by four skylights and a narrow window in the gable end. A central hall with dining room and drawing room on either side fill the ground floor of the barn. Above, bedrooms and bathrooms open off a passageway along the front of the house. The original internal and outside walls have been dry lined to stop damp seeping through the plaster. All the new walls and floors have a solidity that gives a feeling of permanence, often lacking in a modern house. Upstairs the new walls are thicker than the old ones, reinforced with breeze blocks between the insulated plasterboard and stonework. Extra-thick ceiling joists were used to keep the upstairs floors rigid and sound-proofed and at ground level the floor is strategically layered. Over a damp course and concrete

In true country house style, a profusion of cabbage rose chintz decorates the bed and three windows in Sue and Geoffrey Smart's large sunny bedroom. Dappled pink wallpaper echoes the roses.

screen lies a floating floor of thick polystyrene topped with wooded chipboard – providing, in theory, enough insulation to heat the room with a candle. Failing this, there is also gas central heating, open fires and an Aga.

The hall retains some of the barn's original volume although the mood is definitely country house, rather than rustic. It is dominated by a wide curving staircase in Brazilian mahogany and copious folds of flowery chintz that hang at the tall arched window. The drawing room is flooded with light from a large bay window and three full-height sash windows that open on

to the lawn. Mimosa-yellow walls and matching carpet give a summery backdrop to the antique furniture and detailing of the acanthus cornice, carved marble fireplace and deep, white skirting boards.

Despite his cautious budgeting, Geoffrey invested £900 in the extra deep skirting boards. 'The extra cost was justified by the substance they give to a room,' he says. The mouldings between walls and ceiling in every room add definition and also help conceal cracks in the plaster. The doors were specially made to generous dimensions – although Geoffrey wishes they were even thicker. He almost exploded with rage over the windows. After producing a perfect sample, the joiners were commissioned to make all the sash windows. When none of them fitted the Smarts realized they had been shown a superior window from an established joinery firm in Berwick-upon-Tweed. A court case was averted by filling the rattling gaps with layers of paint and double glazing.

The decoration contributes to the settled country house atmosphere. It reflects Sue Smart's eye for colour and design. She is a self-taught painter who decorates tiles, china and lamps with delicate flower and insect motifs. Her love of flowers is evident from the glorious chintz curtains that hang below deep pelmets at every window – except in the dining room where plain raspberry chintz complements the sage-green walls, and in the kitchen with its pine furniture, stencilled friezes and sprigged cotton curtains. Sue and Geoffrey's bedroom above the drawing room has an extravagance of pink cabbage roses. A trellised chintz 'Ludlow' by Ramm, Son and Crocker, decorates the bed and three windows. Dappled pink wallpaper echoes the roses and a plain chintz valance and bedside table-cloths pick out the turquoise of the trellis. An ensuite bathroom continues the pink theme with rosebud-striped walls and curtains which frame the view from the bath into the garden.

From these rooms an arch leads through into a narrow passage with biscuit-coloured walls and carpet; a calm foil to the impact of six billowing chintz curtains patterned with crimson roses and ribbons. Amy and Sophie Smart's flowery bedrooms open off the passage which ends with the large spare room. Here there is more pink with apple-green walls; a Jane Churchill bow wallpaper, with Colefax and Fowler rose and lily 'Lymington' chintz bedspreads and curtains. A child size door in the wall opens into the playroom which also doubles as a spare room for visiting children. As well as toys and an inbuilt Wendy House it contains a ping-pong table that

The hall in the central bay of the barn retains part of its original volume, dominated now by a sweeping mahogany staircase, immaculate joinery and copious folds of chintz

had to be installed through a gap in the floorboards before the room was finished. At the far end a steep staircase leads down to an old dog kennel at the back of the granary where Sue has made herself a studio. Between this and the kitchen there is a small, informal sitting room with an Adam-style fireplace and simple white mouldings against pale-peach walls and furnishings.

The garden was originally an unpromising sheepdip which was filled with builders' rubble during the conversion. But once bulldozed to a level surface, 'it came up like a billiards table,' says Geoffrey. The whole area was laid with meadow turf before herbaceous beds and shrubs were planted. Both the interior and garden have been transformed gradually over a period of six years. Compared to the rapid change from farmbuilding to house the rest of the venture has been time consuming and expensive – but enormously worthwhile. Contemplating the past years from his comfortable sofa, Geoffrey admits, 'It would have been cheaper to bulldoze it all down and start again but then you wouldn't have the character of the place – and, as they say, only fools build houses for wise men to live in . . .'

CWM CAE

STEPHEN AND LUCY RICHARDS

—— ~ ——

When Matthew, Thomas or Emily forget to close doors behind them they can blame their upbringing in a barn. Every holiday, half-term and occasional weekend they exchange Wimbledon for a converted smallholding in west Wales. It is a long drive from London but their father, Stephen, has Welsh roots. He too spent childhood holidays in Wales with his parents who have settled close by – near enough to

keep an eye on the Richards' barn and even mow the grass in summer.

Cwm Cae (meaning valley of fields) stands alone on top of a steep winding lane, surrounded by fields of sheep. It is a T-shaped stone building bedded into the side of a hill. The vertical element is the long barn at right angles to the farmhouse, typical of a Welsh smallholding where animals lived beside their keepers. On a clear day you can see Cader Idris and the peaks of Plynlimon across the Dovey Valley but it is an exposed setting where the elements cannot be ignored. The place has weathered well since the early nineteenth century, built to withstand the constant wind, mist and rain that tend to obscure the view. A characteristic lack of pointing between the stonework allows the wind to dry the rain-filled crevices in the thick, lichened walls. When Stephen and Lucy Richards bought Cwm Cae eight years ago it was immediately habitable but still very much a barn. 'Most of the places we'd looked at were either a complete heap of stone or far too done up already,' recalls Lucy. The farmhouse had stood empty for 40 years but the barn was still in sporadic use when the buildings were bought in 1973 by an architect, Roderick James. With his wife Gillie, he converted the barn, salvaged the farmhouse and combined them into a rambling home, full of innovative ideas and detail. The Richards inherited Roderick's inspiration which has needed minimum alteration or upkeep.

The barn is the heart of the house. You walk through the front door into a long, galleried living space that looks down over the kitchen and dining areas which were originally the cattle and pig stores. 'It seems appropriate that our dining room was originally a pigsty,' observes Stephen.

The building is set into the hillside and so both floors give the impression of being at ground level. The uneven slate roof adds great character from the outside: on the dining room and kitchen side, it slopes down to a gutter just above window level, giving a look that is somehow top heavy, as if the whole building is weighed down by its roof.

The upper level of the barn is an open living space, 30 foot long with a pitched ceiling supported by open roof trusses,

substantial oak beams and posts. The end wall, adjoining the farmhouse, is inset with an unusual truncated cruck pattern – 'An architectural feature, otherwise known as Welsh provincial?' suggests Stephen. Much of the framework predates the building, having served as eighteenth-century ship timbers, dismantled from local ports along the River Dovey. They interlock like easy jigsaws of wooden pegs and notches, scored with Roman numerals, hieroglyphics, and later contributions from woodworm and insects.

A massive stone fireplace faces the half-cruck wall, adding a square chimney to the roof line. It creates a sitting area at one end of the room, furnished with wicker chairs and sofas. Until the flames start leaping, the warmest perch is a stone seat carved out of the fireplace. The other end of the barn is sparsely furnished. There is enough room to string a swing and hammock from the beams which are 12 foot above the ground. The quantity of exposed timbers, accentuated by a mountain of logs in a recess by the fireplace, dominates the atmosphere.

Decoration is intentionally simple. Against the white stone walls and pitch pine floor (salvaged from Liverpool docks) there are restricted splashes of primary colours and an occasional ethnic pattern. Unlined Ikat curtains hang at the windows where rough stone sills measure the depth of the walls. The window frames are painted scarlet, matching a line of cupboards fitted between the beams above the wooden balcony. Below these hang unobtrusive cream curtains which can be pulled across at night.

There was no direct access between floors as, originally, hay from the barn would have been thrown to the trough down below. Now stone steps cut through the horizontal wall plate and lead down to the lower level. This is a narrow version of the upper floor lit by a row of windows set into the rebuilt kitchen wall. The original animal vents have been kept and glazed, making peep holes into a downstairs bedroom. The continuity of the quarry-tiled floor and white walls is interrupted by a low-beamed arch, standing on a truncated telegraph pole that divides the dining area and kitchen. The dining part has cheerful green window frames

PREVIOUS PAGE, *Cwm Cae appears to grow out of the hillside*
RIGHT, *Stone steps with quarry-tiled treads lead from the kitchen and dining area up to the main barn space*

and matching lampshades which hang low over the table. In keeping with the barn's character, the kitchen appears suitably low-tech but is well equipped with oak units, sycamore worktops and a double sink tiled with sunflowers. Noise and cooking smells are shielded from above by a clear glass partition fixed behind the balcony – a windscreen like device that contains the kitchen element without losing its openness.

The inherited Rayburn has been replaced by a central heating system which is turned on through the winter; a necessary outlay after Stephen and Lucy had to cope with a flood and burst pipes from a distance. It keeps the interior dry and welcoming after an impromptu dash from London.

There is access to the farmhouse from both levels of the barn, through the kitchen and by a door knocked through the adjoining cruck-framed wall. Its ground floor has a cosy sitting room, a playroom-cum-workshop and indistinguishable extension with an extra bedroom and greenhouse. Sleeping accommodation is shared between both buildings; the Richards in the farmhouse and visitors in the barn. Converted from a cart and tractor store at the gable end, the three spare bedrooms and bathroom are full of character with beamed sloping ceilings. Steps behind the fireplace lead up to a tent-like room with walls and a pitched roof painted scarlet between the rafters. Complete with a trap door in the floor, it makes a perfect child-size den and setting for Matthew's and Thomas's clockwork trains. The spare bedroom below, which backs on to the barn's fireplace, is heated by a Heath Robinson copper wall plate that diffuses warmth into the room. The whole building is full of such logical, economical systems. In the farmhouse a pipe from the bathroom carries hot water to a storage tank which is used to heat the greenhouse. Perhaps that is why the strawberry plants, peach tree and parsley do so well.

Visions of the barn as a permanent home have faded because of commitments to the children's education and Stephen's law practice. But because of the strong family ties, the Richards do not feel like outsiders. Not that there is any hostility in this part of Wales. The extra income in the shops is welcomed and the locals seem pleased that an otherwise derelict building can be revived by migrants from the south. As well as marrying a Welshman, Lucy is connected to the area by keen membership of the Montgomeryshire London Society.

Outside, the land slopes down towards fields of sheep. Neighbours are in short supply, but the garden is scattered with aesthetic diversions for children and grown-ups. There are slate-roofed Wendy Houses, a pond for collecting frog spawn, a tree house and a collapsed pigsty that shelters hardy perennials from the wind. Looming over all this is a hexagonal wooden tower, standing on three oak tree trunks. Its original purpose, as a canvas-sailed Cretan windmill, was to generate electricity but now it has become an eccentric summerhouse and retreat where Stephen and Lucy take turns in visiting to enjoy its apple-green walls and panoramic view across Wales.

SEAGULL BARN
RODERICK AND GILLIE JAMES

~

Having lived in a barn it is difficult to go back to a house without feeling cramped. Roderick and Gillie James are committed to barns. They began their married life in one perched on top of a Welsh mountain, then moved on to restore a second derelict barn in Gloucestershire. Their sons, Daniel, Ben and Woody have grown up in open spaces created by their imaginative, practical parents; accustomed from an early age to a quality of light and space and the freedom of one lofty room. It was not surprising that when the Jameses moved again they had to have a barn.

Instead of being drawn to an agricultural wreck, they fell in love with a magical corner of South Devon. Seagull House stood above a creek hidden from the outside world by a maze of high-hedged lanes. The lack of barn was no deterrent. There was enough room beside the house – planning permission willing – to build a barn that would increase the living space and eventually join up with the house. So, armed with past experience, Roderick's talent as an architect, and Gillie's for colour and design, they set to work on building a green oak, timber-framed barn.

The result proves the time-lessness of vernacular architecture. It is obviously a new building but the simple design and indigenous materials imply that the barn could have been there for centuries. It fits perfectly into the landscape; 'Everyone from the postman to local millionaire says it's the most attractive new building they have seen for years,' admits Gillie with uncharacteristic triumph. The barn has a robust originality that borrows

Roderick and Gillie's carved birds perch above the green skirting board on shelves slotted between curved wall braces

from tradition without being bound by it. The curving green oak timbers, which came mostly from local trees blown down in the hurricane of 1987, have a deliberately rough finish, sand-blasted like driftwood, to give a pale grainy surface. Unlike the interior of most traditional barns there is an impact of freshness and colour; of blond oak against weathered pink walls, terra-cotta roof boarding and milky-green floors.

The structure follows the pattern of a traditional Devon barn; 48 foot long, divided between four bays with triangular roof trusses. The two central bays have no tie beams which emphasizes the barn's height and lightness. Balustraded galleries at each end add to the living space and create an atmosphere more domestic than ecclesiastical. But besides local tradition there is also a strong New England influence on the design and colour scheme. 'It's the whole feeling of the place that inspires us,' explains Roderick, 'the clapboard houses, the coast, the water, the boats and colour of it all.' On their last visit to America the Jameses discovered a curious similarity between their tip of Devon and Connecticut – the same tree-lined creeks, salt water, air and fierce sunlight that fades bright colour. There is also the satisfaction of barn raising in the Pennsylvanian Amish tradition. And from the West Coast, they are influenced by a Californian approach to architecture; 'The innovative, funky, tree-rooty style'.

But what is it about barns that captivates Roderick and Gillie? 'We like the space, the quality of light – and the way people relate to each other in a barn,' says Roderick. 'You don't get involved in "Arab elbow culture". There's enough room to maintain a full arm's length distance from people.' Before it was finished or properly furnished the whole family gravitated across the courtyard from house to barn. Roderick's large desk was quietly commandeered by Gillie as a tranquil place to sew her patchwork quilt. 'The space in a barn makes you feel peaceful and relaxed,' explains Daniel who is 15. For Woody, aged nine, 'It is a good place for carpentry'.

Having built their barn, the Jameses would unhesitatingly choose a new structure in preference to an old one. Besides the vast financial advantage, a new barn can be tailored to a certain size, shape or height. 'You are not having to take it all apart to put back what you want,' says Gillie. 'There is no endless dirt and dust or clearing up.' The only mess was an aesthetic silver sand beach on the floor after the structure had been sandblasted.

The delight they take in their barn has fired Roderick's new venture. With two partners based in Gloucestershire and Wiltshire he has formed a company, Carpenter Oak and Woodland, that produces green-oak barn frames in any size and shape. The basic frame, built by a team of specialist carpenters, is infilled with regional materials – stone, brick, clapboard, glass – that complement the local landscape and vernacular architecture. Roderick believes the robust character of these new buildings matches the qualities that made an old barn so special. 'In the past we've always felt it *had* to be old to be good, so we've struggled to clean up beams and treat woodworm. Most barns as houses are destroyed. What is the point of having a barn, then dividing it into a series of boxes? Now, for a fraction of the cost and effort, a green oak frame can provide a real barn space as an extension to a house.'

The basic frame of the Jameses' barn, built as a prototype by Carpenter Oak and Woodland, cost them £23,500. (Roof slates, complete insulation, plasterboarding and glazing added another £10,000 to the final cost.) In five days it grew from a large heap of wood into a deceptively simple-looking structure which was then assembled on a brick base by Roderick and three carpenters.

He is confident that the barn will stand for centuries. Each joint, matched and numbered like a puzzle, is pegged together with dovetail and tenon joints which lock tightly as the wood shrinks with age. There is no superfluous detail in the design. All the beams, rafters, braces and purlins are essential to the barn structure. The roof is decorative but functional, patterned by curved wind braces between the purlins. As there are no stone end walls, the wind braces are needed to keep the building rigid and prevent the roof from tilting.

The quantity of daylight is an obvious priority. Glass panels in the gabled entrance porch continue along two entire walls, giving the impression of a colonial conservatory (glass barns are another project on Roderick's drawing board). Additional windows have a practical as well as visual purpose. At one end of the barn narrow windows beside the chimney make pitching holes for dropping logs down to the fireplace. A log-piled recess is a James hallmark, continued from past interiors; 'After two barns you know what works,' says Gillie. Another favourite detail on the other side of the fireplace was a bed for catnapping – replaced here by an upright piano, painted beige and rust by Gillie so that it merges into the walls.

At the other end of the barn a tall pointed window brightens the whole roof structure. Shafts of light also stream into the gallery from a glass door that opens off a tennis court behind the barn. From here the boys can creep in unnoticed to startle their parents and friends below. Opposite the entrance is a narrow dormer window set between the rafters that gives a 'Swallows and Amazons' view of boats in the creek. 'Tiny windows give a view which is as dramatic, if not more so, than a large one,' believes Roderick. 'They frame a small part of the landscape and give a changing picture as you move around.' He disregards any objection to dormer windows interrupting the roof line. 'The thing I like seeing from my bath is the dormer, not the skylights – although I do like the light they provide inside the barn.' Four skylights are arranged in pairs just below the clay roof ridge. 'By having them right at the top you don't get the glare which detracts from the roof structure.' On grey days, sunlight and shadow can

Old and contemporary spongeware pottery is displayed on shelves fixed over an old wooden grain bin from a farm in Gloucestershire – an arrangement that looks like a wide Welsh dresser

be improvised by 20 bright spotlights angled in all directions along the purlins in the roof.

The warm colours in the barn appear ready-bleached by the abundant natural light. A mix of mushroom pink, brick red and sage recall an Andrew Wyeth painting – perhaps a New England still life – or, more intentionally, a scene by Carl Larsson whose palette is an inspiration to Gillie and Roderick. On the walls, plaster between the studs and curved oak braces remains its original putty pink. The roof boarding behind the rafters has been painted with a warm terracotta emulsion applied straight on to the oak. The milky green floor was created by an experimental technique devised by Gillie; the softwood boards were painted with three coats of Dulux Camouflage, followed by a layer of clear varnish. The colour scheme changes slightly with each barn, but the Jameses keep the same bold furniture; two massive Conran sofas covered in fawn striped cotton; directors' canvas chairs and slatted ash recliners by David Colwell that echo the curved lines in the barn's structure.

'It's incredible in here at night,' enthuses Gillie. The mellow colours spread a warm glow through the barn which is accentuated by spotlights angled to illuminate the pale oak and bare glass walls. To avoid startling themselves with their own reflections, an external spotlight shines on trees and plants outside the barn. 'It stops it feeling too bogey in the dark!' says Gillie.

There is enough room for Roderick's office at one end, equipped with fax machine, photocopier and telephones.

'They don't feel too intrusive in a space like this,' he says. 'Normally people would think it very odd to have such machines in a sitting room – but they don't seem to comment on it here.' Gillie's favourite among 'the ugly machines' is a hi-fi system. 'Music sounds wonderful in here because the accoustics are so good,' she says. The technology content contrasts with the robust furniture and fittings, and hand-crafted ornaments. 'You can't have anything that is too finished or precious in such a rough setting – it looks all wrong,' says Roderick. A collection of antique wooden sailing boats and American decoy ducks perch on simple oak shelves pegged between the wall studs. A prized vessel that belonged to Roderick's great-grandfather stands on an old wooden grain bin salvaged from a farm in Gloucestershire. With shelves above, it looks like a giant dresser, decked with antique china and spongeware pottery. Roderick's desk is homemade – a Douglas Fir table top laid on filing cabinets – and was used for the Jameses' barn-warming dinner.

Among the antique decoys there are more modern shore birds and ducks, carved by Roderick and painted by Gillie. They represent a venture which grew from Gillie's own collection into a commercial enterprise. Now both interests – birds and boats – are pursued beside the creek in a timber-framed boathouse with an oak shingled roof built, not surprisingly, by Roderick. In one half he restores old boats and overhauls his precious 1936 gaff ketch. The other half is a workshop where seagulls, ducks and herons come to life from soft lumps of wood.

Roderick's office merges against a background of green oak, plants and glass. The gallery above is reached by ladder or through a glass door in the roof.

SAWMILLS

CLARE AND RICHARD HALSTEAD

———~———

Tucked away in Montgomeryshire stands a small working hamlet called Sawmills, a red-brick settlement of 21 houses and outbuildings, founded in 1870 by a prosperous Liverpool banker. Over a century later Clare and Richard Halstead have settled here with their own rural industry – a gallery of country art and craft.

They live and work in a Victorian farm building in the heart of Sawmills. After living in London, Yorkshire and West Wales, the Halsteads longed to find somewhere in need of complete restoration. They searched mid-Wales, then in 1982 just as it came on the market they discovered the perfect challenge. It was an L-shaped building that had grown from a seventeenth-century barn into stables, cowshed and cartstore in 1870. Most of the early, grey stone had been dwarfed by the Victorian additions. The barn roof had been removed, its walls dismantled and rebuilt using the local brick which by now had mellowed to a warm coral. This colour is emphasized by a slate-grey roof, blue-brick lintels above the windows and arches around the doors.

Sale negotiations took place in the stables, occupied at the time by a goat, although previously it had housed ponies, carthorses and traps. The original barn at right angles to the stables had become the cowshed, partitioned into stalls and calving pens, with a hayloft above. Beyond that was another hayloft with space below for farm carts.

The Halsteads' first priority was to make the stables habitable then, when time and money allowed, to overflow into the cowshed and finally to convert the cartshed. For 18

RIGHT, *The tackroom has been divided into a passage and bathroom. A carthorse stable provides an essential larder and storeroom*

BELOW, *The Victorian blue brick arches remain beside a new projecting window that adds light and space to the living quarters*

months they camped in the cowshed while the stables were converted. Apart from professional help to build a second chimney and dig the drains, all the design and physical work was done by Clare and Richard. Neither had had any experience except for a mutual background in art (Richard in sculpture, Clare in dress design) which gave them plenty of visual inspiration. But even in a small space, planning the layout was far more difficult than they envisaged. 'We found the hardest part was the lack of obvious orientation,' explains Richard. 'There was no starting point, nothing forcing the kitchen to be here or there.'

On the drawing board, the stable block was a rectangle, 33 foot long and 12 foot wide with four north-facing openings on to a concrete yard – a large cart entrance, two arched doorways and one small window. There was a central wall which divided the traps from horses and a cramped pigeon loft at one end lit by two tiny arches. The only domesticated area was a tack room in the crook of the L with an open fireplace, panelled walls and blue-brick floor.

What they have created is a contemporary version of one-room cottage life. It is infinitely prettier and more comfortable but has echoes of basic country life where everything happened in one room. Here, with great organization, a sleeping loft, sitting area, dining table, office space and kitchen have all been fitted in. 'The fact that we haven't gone crazy in five years is a tribute to this way of living,' says Clare. 'It is very workable, although I do long for more space.'

The conversion involved more renovation than rebuild-

ing. The stables were damp but structurally sound with solid walls and a mostly intact slate roof. After removing the internal partition, the main job was to lift a sodden brick floor and replace it with concrete laid over a damp course. The old bricks have been recycled and used inside as steps and outside for flowerbed surrounds in the gravelled courtyard by the stables. Because of its agricultural status the internal walls were built with inferior bricks, but fortunately their softness was an asset. The combination of fading coral-brick, pointed with lime mortar, was worth preserving. Although sand-blasting would have been less arduous it would have threatened the soft colour, so Clare spent two months brushing off layers of limewash. Once revealed, the bricks were left in a natural state to breathe and emphasise their character. Although building experts were horrified by the lack of insulation the stables feel warm and dry. A re-enamelled black, 1930s Aga heats the kitchen area backed-up by a small navy woodburner at the sitting-room end. Its exposed flue works as a vertical radiator, heating ground and sleeping space above.

Clare and Richard's bedroom is tucked between the eaves like a miniature Swiss chalet. By lowering the loft floor they gained just enough headroom to stand upright in the middle – but it would not suit anyone with claustrophic tendencies. Ventilation comes through two arched pigeon holes with carved shutters that accentuate the cuckoo clock effect. Instead of glass they are fitted with wire netting to curb the nocturnal pounces of Cato, the Siamese cat. Clare and Richard climb up to bed using a wooden ladder with well worn rungs, which was acquired in exchange for a bottle of Martini from a local farmer. It matches the rustic pine balcony that prevents them from toppling out of bed, an adaptation from an old manger that was fitted along the stable wall. There is just enough room for a double bed, covered with one of Clare's delicate quilts and a music centre. Despite the cosiness they look forward to converting the cowshed loft into a larger bedroom, ensuite bathroom, dressing room and sewing room.

As all the doors and windows in the stables face north, it was essential to let in as much daylight as possible (a condition of the planning permission was to keep the original openings). The large cart doors at the sitting-room end were replaced by a projecting window that widens the ground space and creates an integral conservatory. The black-tiled area under the window, higher than floor level, makes a perfect spot for the plants that jostle for space with the photocopier. Like the outside of the building, the door and windows are framed by blue-brick lintels and arches that add to the original textures. The solid wall opposite the windows, interrupted by small vents, is half stone, half brick, showing where the stables originally evolved from the old stone wall. Cream-painted stonework juts out from the brick above like a rustic dado, making a ledge for storage jars, books, piles of magazines and a suitable backdrop for primitive pictures.

A narrow door, knocked through the end wall, leads into the old tack room which has now been divided into a bathroom and passageway. The tack room fireplace has been blocked off but much of the panelling has been re-used on the walls, cupboards and against the bath. The passage doubles as a hallway with boots and baskets lined up along the blue-brick floor.

Instead of bridles, hats and coats hang on the giant tack room pegs beside a tartan-curtained window. Further on, behind a jade-green door, a solitary carthorse stable has been transformed into a store for food, china, glass and cookbooks – an essential room that explains the lack of clutter in the main living space. As well as recycling original materials, the Halsteads made the most of all local resources. Rotting windows and wall panels were replaced with identical versions from demolition yards, 'dug out of the snow for bargain prices,' recalls Clare. The marble-topped kitchen cupboards were made by Richard from old pine panels bought in a Shrewsbury junk shop. A large wooden Bible cupboard, revived by a jade colour wash to match the storeroom door, cost them £10 from a local farmhouse.

Although camping in a calving pen was surprisingly warm – animal buildings were often dug below ground level to keep a constant temperature – it was primitive and uncomfortable. After living with cobbled floors, polythene-draped walls and no running water, Clare and Richard longed for more civilized and decorative surroundings in the stables. Swedish, Gustavian style inspired an interior of fresh colour and robust texture, mixing blue and white cottons with bricks, stone and rush matting. 'I like using traditional materials in a contemporary way,' explains Clare. Crisp gingham curtains hang from wooden poles, matching the cornflower-blue sprigged tablecloth, the cushions on the country chairs and along the pine bench against the wall. These simple furnishings are in keeping with the bell-shaped lampshades – bought years ago from Oxfam – the baskets and dried flowers hanging from the beams. At the sitting-room end, comfortable armchairs, books, magazines, pictures and plants compete for space with a narrow desk and office shelves.

While the conversion was in progress the Halsteads had little time or energy left to shiver over their art in a makeshift studio above the cartshed. For a time Richard drew houses on commission and Clare produced quilted cushion kits. The idea for a gallery grew from the need to interrupt such rustic isolation with human contact. There was also a lack of anywhere local to buy original presents – untwee pottery, pictures, baskets, cards, jewellery or toys. After looking for premises in Newtown they realized the best solution would be to use their own property and convert the cowshed into a gallery and shop. 'It was a bit of a shot in the dark, especially as

The living-room end of the stables is shared between comfortable seating and office space. Clare and Richard sleep in the pigeon loft.

we are well off the main road,' says Clare, 'but people have a nice surprise when they get here – and they keep coming back.'

The gallery occupies the ground floor of the cattlesheds which had to be gutted and then given a new loft floor using joists from the old roof rafters. Christened Country Works, it was an immediate success, opening in May 1987 with an exhibition of Shropshire basketry. The formula of monthly shows of art, ceramics, textiles and sculpture by local and national artists in a craft shop setting works well. Changing exhibitions is a way of attracting regular visitors. Some come from the neighbourhood, others from the North and the Midlands. There is an emphasis on products with country associations. Any card, mug, or picture showing a sheep, duck or goose is a guaranteed best seller. But Clare and Richard are discriminating buyers who avoid anything predictable.

The gallery is more like a rural branch of The Conran Shop than the average craft shop. Where else in Wales could you buy an Edwardian nut-picking stick, American folk art cards or an antique patchwork quilt?

MAYBOLE FARM
KATE AND OLIVER ANDERSON

—~—

After driving through Scottish towns lined with stern grey houses the Girvan Valley appears as an unexpected oasis. Suddenly the landscape changes, the road narrows and winds into gentle green countryside that leads to Maybole Farm. Its pink stone walls stand out like a welcoming scoop of strawberry icecream, in frivolous contrast to the grey Ayrshire stone. The farm buildings have been pink for as long as the locals can

remember. Kate and Oliver Anderson kept the tradition then added deep turquoise paint to the windows, doors and gutters. Were it not for the dark Ballachulish slate roof the effect would be more Mediterranean than Scottish.

Maybole Farm is laid out around three sides of a square; a central cowbyre flanked by living quarters and stables. The previous occupants were two elderly spinsters who lived between the dairy and granary in a corner of the building. When the Andersons bought the property in 1971 it was in need of serious repair but had the makings of an eccentric family house. They were the first family to live there. As a tenanted farm it had been occupied by a series of bachelor labourers before being sold to the spinsters. None had believed in home improvements. Time indoors was spent by the range in an all-purpose kitchen next to the dairy, while the cows had more privileged accommodation in the adjoining byre. Outside, the surrounding farmyard was in a revolting state. Today, the only remaining legacy is a rowan tree that grew amongst the midden of tyres and broken bottles.

The architecture is typical of Scottish vernacular style; a nineteenth-century, single storey building with a first floor added in the roof for a granary and tack room. These became bedrooms, but the Andersons decided to expand the ground space by knocking through into the byre, then into the stables. Perhaps because no family had ever lived there, the farm lacked a room large enough for entertaining or somewhere for children to play. The 40-foot cow byre was the obvious answer, especially as it was already part of the house, separated only by an internal wall. The original dimensions were kept but it needed windows and a floor laid over the cobbled stone. The only opening, double doors at the far end, became a window. 'I don't remember about planning permission in those days,' says Kate. 'We had good builders and told them to carry on through.'

The byre was open to the roof but a low-beamed ceiling was put in to give it cosier proportions and less cold air to heat.

Next to the dairy, the old kitchen with a flagstoned floor and welcoming green walls has become Oliver's office. Like their predecessors, the Andersons find it a room where people like to gather.

With the stage curtain drawn to one side, the far end of the
40-foot byre is used as an informal games room and
temporary despatch office for mail-order smoked salmon

'We did it all ourselves – as you can see by the curve of the ceiling,' remarks Kate. She comes from Hampshire but feels part of Ayrshire having lived there for almost 20 years. In spite of its apparent remoteness, the area is full of migrants from the south. 'It's not lonely at all. There are lots of interesting people around, not all dyed-in-the-wool Scots!' she says. Oliver is a local. He grew up in Ayrshire but left Scotland for the army, returning home to farm and run an agricultural contracting business. Kate, mother of seven-year-old Nancy, looks far too young to have a grown-up son and daughter as well. Her relaxed manner conceals an enterprising spirit.

During the July golf tournament at Troon she provides bed and breakfast in the stable wing for rich Australians or Americans. 'It all helps pay for the next house improvement,' she explains. Another sideline engulfs one end of the byre. Before Christmas it doubles as despatch department for The Salmon Pool, a mail order business supplying local smoked and ginger cured salmon and gravadlax. 'We have fridges stuck in every corner of the room. The only trouble is the smell!'

After Christmas the despatch end resumes its role as an informal games area with a full-size ping-pong table and tomato-red walls crowded with bookshelves and sporting pictures. The wooden floor was not planned. It is the result of a flood that ruined the original full length carpet but helps set the scene at Christmas time or at children's parties when the space becomes a stage for plays and charades. To add to the theatrical atmosphere there are green stage curtains to draw across the byre between acts. Performances are watched from the drawing room end where people gravitate towards a fireplace with a white stone surround and plain wooden mantelpiece.

The room has the atmosphere of a comfortable shooting lodge. White stone walls make a backdrop for a generous number of unmatching sofas, armchairs and antique furniture. Its substantial scale and quantity give a crowded friendly atmosphere - an inviting place for winter afternoons by the fire. There is an effective lack of symmetry or status given to the elegant furniture. Regency tables and cabinets jostle against Georgian bureaux, bookcases and tallboys. Surfaces are piled with leather bound books, family photographs, wooden boxes and lamps. A Regency mahogany table, with splayed legs, stands in the centre of the room, ready for family parties and vases of poppies from the garden. 'We've been very lucky indeed with inherited furniture,' says Kate, 'especially as we couldn't have anything modern in here. Of course I would love to redo this room with an array of wonderful furnishings – but we'll get there one day,' she adds. Finances have been swallowed up by roof repairs and attempts to curtail the water that resisted a damp course in the byre walls.

The byre is connected to the house by a door that leads into a tomato red passage with a boarded dado, striped red and green. Its entrance is guarded by a pair of crossed swords from Oliver's regiment, the Argyll and Sutherland Highlanders. A snuggery fills the old dairy where more antiques find space beside armchairs battered by Nancy and a terrier puppy.

The granary above is Kate and Oliver's bedroom, reached by stairs from the entrance hall instead of the original steps from the dairy. A traditional farmhouse kitchen occupies a surprisingly large space below the tack room. When the Andersons arrived, it housed a solitary tin bath for an occasional scrub. Obviously more time was spent in the cosier old kitchen where the cast-iron range remains, black against emerald-green walls. It is now Oliver's office where paperwork, spread over a long table, is joined by meals, toys and household clutter. Like the old days, it is a room where people and objects like to gather.

CASTLE BARN
JAMES AND EMMA FAIRFAX

~

Converting a barn into a castle seemed a logical idea to James and Emma Fairfax. Evidence that a castle had once stood on or near the site of their barn was too strong to ignore. The farmhouse and outbuildings have always been called The Castle. Its setting was strategic, built at a vantage point in the dip of a Welsh valley just below the skyline. Above all, the impressive structure and raw materials, the deep stone walls, flagstone floors, ventilation holes like arrow slits, suggested the barn's early origins.

When the Fairfaxes bought Castle Barn six years ago it included a run down Victorian house, a building of no special beauty that did not appeal as a new home. Fortunately it was pronounced irredeemable by their architect and the Fairfaxes were given permission to pull it down. This left resources and raw materials to concentrate on the barn and outbuildings which stood in a welcoming enclave around what is now a herringboned-brick courtyard and herb garden.

Apart from a strong sense of history the barn was no architectural masterpiece and didn't demand exact preservation. The Fairfaxes needed to create a home that suited their busy farm life, three teenage children, dogs, cats and ducks. 'It would have been a travesty to turn it into a "des res", but it did need to be tamed and domesticated,' Emma explains. She has an aversion to what she sees as an epidemic of barn conversions but hopes their own still counts as a working building – an integral part of the 200-acre sheep and herb farm run by James. 'There always has to be room for orphan lambs in the kitchen,' she insists.

Castle Barn stands at a vantage point in the dip of a valley, fortified by three crenellated towers. Even the uncurtained windows expanded from the animals' breathing vents could have been arrow slits.

The barn is an expression of Emma's obsession with building and design. She is untrained in the technicalities but has an all consuming flair for anything visual. James, an economist who left the Treasury to farm, lets her pursue what she calls 'her madness'. Creating a castle from a simple stone building was a challenge that fired her imagination and infectiously romantic nature. Ideas accumulated gradually as details of towers, battlements and Gothick archways were jotted down on old envelopes. The project began with an architect but financial limits meant the Fairfaxes remained in control, working first with surveyors then builders. At the time they were living on a farm down the road so could be on site to watch the progress. Disaster struck early on when the barn collapsed. It lacked proper foundations and inaccurate digging undermined the structure before it could be properly underpinned. For a whole year progress was delayed. Their only compensation was the insurance money paid out for negligence.

The castle element took the shape of a square tower with battlements at one end of the barn which successfully doubled the living space. Crenellations also sprout from a central turret and projecting bay window which unite both sections into an eccentric whole. Beside their striking façade, the fortifications endorse the air of unthreatened stability which engulfs Castle Barn. The view of hills, fields and woodland is unbroken by any other building or sign of life. Instead of a moat, the castle looks on to a wild flower meadow, harvested for its seed each summer.

The changing landscape is a

powerful influence on Emma's design and it was of the utmost importance that the castle blended harmoniously with its surroundings – nothing should jar or look too obviously new. To match the original stonework of the barn, similar blocks were cut from a wet stone quarry in the Forest of Dean. Stone for the tower came from a collapsed priory in Wales which was bought as a ruin, then dismantled and transported in pieces. The demolished Victorian farmhouse also provided a valuable source of materials. Old bricks, floorboards, roof tiles and timbers were recycled whenever possible for financial and visual reasons.

Emma believes in the value of constraints. 'There is no such thing in building as a blank page. There is always something you have to make use of. I would have exploded with excitement if it could have been started from scratch.' For such a perfectionist the most time consuming part was finding appropriate, yet inexpensive materials. She has become an expert at creating illusions, giving cheaper chestnut floorboards and banisters the look of oak, using exterior front doors inside to balance the scale of a room.

The front entrance was designed around an imposing Gothick oak door from an architectural salvage company. Alterations and additions were planned around the original barn's proportions. The animals' breathing vents, expanded into deep-silled narrow windows, are supplemented by large sash and bay windows. Each room has been designed to make the most of natural daylight so that even dull February days are brightened by watery sunlight that shafts through uncurtained vents. The contrast between large and small brings the landscape inside, framing a glimpse from the kitchen table or a cinematic view from the triple bay window in the great hall.

A feeling of light and space reflects the barn spirit but there is an uncharacteristic intimacy about the place. Doors that lead along stone flagged passages conceal the rooms from immediate view. 'The whole place is about surprise, doors that open on to different scenes,' explains Emma. The ground floor of the barn divides into three connecting rooms: the kitchen, hall and drawing

The barn kitchen, an integral part of the farm, is crowded with an aesthetic mix of decorative and practical objects. The duck-egg blue walls continue into a more formal dining room that opens into the garden.

room. On a small scale the Great Hall, as the Fairfaxes call it, is the most barn-like. It spans the full width and height of the building. There is a massive stone fireplace, pale grey walls, a collection of family portraits and a staircase to a gallery above. Here comfort prevails. Thermally insulated walls, central heating and an efficient Jet Master inside the grey-stone fireplace warm the room. There are inviting wing armchairs, and a refectory table and chairs set in the bay from where there is an optimum view of the wild flower meadow.

The drawing room is smaller and indulgently feminine. It recalls a Regency morning room where gentle colour makes a backdrop for elegant bookcases, slipper chairs, gilded mirrors and fresh flowers. The summery atmosphere was inspired by an evocative Victorian painting that hangs between two deep sash windows, picturing a child gazing wistfully into the garden on a hot sunny day. The furniture is elaborate and so the decoration is kept simple. The pale, putty wall colour is echoed in the cream-striped moiré curtains that hang from white wooden poles in the sash windows. Both are linked by a delicate ribbon border which gives a narrow cornice below the ceiling. The small fireplace backing on to the central chimney block is painted white, although Emma plans some *trompe-l'oeil* decoration.

In the kitchen the scene changes to a Carl Larsson painting full of intense colour. Like most kitchens it is a working room but there is harmony between the decorative and practical parts. Duck-egg blue – off-the-peg colour toned down with a touch of black and brown – makes an original setting for a collection of Staffordshire figures, antique jugs and everyday Delft china, lined up on shelves made from old floorboards. Saucepans perch on an old oak beam above the Aga. White tiles behind a double sink are interspersed with antique flower-patterned tiles. Old-fashioned birdcages and candelabra, strung from the ceiling, add to the eclectic atmosphere.

Originally, meals were eaten at the round pine table but a dining room extension added to one corner of the room has expanded the size and scale of the kitchen. It also introduces valuable light from full length

windows and French doors that open on to a sheltered terrace. The duck-egg blue scheme has been carried through to unite both rooms and combined with a jade-green door and stained pine floorboards.

Upstairs, light airy bedrooms – two in the barn, three in the tower – are dominated by large windows and floor-level vents, 'so you can lie in bed and watch the sheep below,' says Emma. Beside a whitewashed bedroom, decorated with favourite flower paintings and rows of jugs, Emma has a retreat in the tower beyond the children's bedrooms. Here, removed from their comings and goings and from the activities of the farm, she writes and plans, surrounded by her collections of children's books, teddy bears, shells, dolls' houses, spongeware pottery and many more jugs.

While James farms, Emma runs her business cultivating half an acre of flowers which she then dries and sells. Helped by a grant for small rural industries, the byres and sheds on each side of the courtyard have been converted into a studio, drying and storage rooms. Bunches of rosebuds, delphiniums, cornflowers, larkspur, alchemilla and meadow grasses festoon the ceilings, waiting to be entwined into swags or rustic baskets. Emma's flower arrangements are exquisite: stunning mixtures of fresh and dried, exotic and everyday, each one emphasizing her love of flowers. It is a passion that inspires her to keep fresh blooms in the deep freeze, just for the joy of seeing them out of season. More for pleasure than business, Emma grows every variety of tulip which colour the garden from early April to June. Striped Rembrandts reminiscent of a Brueghel painting bloom amongst sage and thymes in a formal herb garden in the courtyard. Black Kyoga ducks are another pleasure – a modest slug-eating army that guard the castle like mobile sentries.

The Great Hall is the most barn-like of all the rooms. Here shades of grey are dappled by light from the triple bay window and a chandelier that hangs from a twisted silk ribbon.

SHEEPHOUSE BARN

RICHARD AND TISH FIELDEN

~

Sheephouse Barn was lot number seven in a Somerset farm auction, sold after the farmhouse and five lots of land. Even four years ago it was expected to reach an inflated price until prospectors realized there was no guarantee of planning permission. Architect Richard Fielden and his wife Tish had fallen for the long stone barn set into the steep hill of a favourite valley near

Bath. It was part of a run-down dairy farm that had outgrown its site. The farmer and milking herd had moved on, keeping the barns and outbuildings for storage. The surrounding land was of a poor quality, suitable only for rough grazing on fields too steep to plough, and abandoned to wild flowers and deer.

The barn was not a listed building but when Richard Fielden discovered timber wind braces hidden behind the hay, he knew it had been overlooked by the authorities. Four pairs of wind braces (angled timbers between the rafters and purlins) in the roof structure revealed the building's age and significance. As they were rare after 1610, the barn was rightfully listed and the chance of planning permission increased. The Fieldens took a gamble and bought the barn cheaply at auction, competing against one like-minded bidder.

They won their case to convert the barn only at the third attempt when the planners realized it was a matter of collapse or conversion. 'Given that the barn was falling down there was definitely no other use for it,' explains Tish. As an architect, Richard feels torn between the purist desire to leave old buildings alone or find a sympathetic use to prolong their life. 'The character of a barn full of straw, open to the wind is quite different from a barn made into a house. With a conversion, however hard you try to retain the atmosphere of an old farm building, it will still be artificial.' But there is no disputing that the shell of a barn gives an architect flexibility to create a unique living space: 'If I *could* have found an equivalent site in an equivalent position I would have liked to build a house, but conversion does offer great potential,' says Richard.

The Fieldens felt great responsibility to their barn, believed to be the oldest in the area. It was built around 1520 on land owned by Bath Abbey for use as a monastic staple, an outbuilding where crops were stored before threshing. With such a historic pedigree, the Fieldens were determined to make the change from barn to house as unobtrusive as possible. They made only four new external openings, expanding the rest from original doors and ventilation slits. A window added in the far gable end is invisible from the road and so the barn maintains an agricultural front.

New wooden frames, lintels and doors merge discreetly into the walls, muted by grey stain that suggests old stone mullions. But authenticity blends with comfort; the window panes are triple glazed with draughtproof seals.

Changes to the interior were also conservative, following Richard's theory that 'the art of conversion is to change the building as little as possible – which is also better news for the bank balance.' His philosophy was helped by the barn's layout which already suggested a rambling open-plan house consisting as it did of six bays interrupted by a hayloft with stables at one end, a cowshed, and cobbled animal pen at the other. The only structural addition was a bedroom floor on the same level as the hayloft. Otherwise the interior has been fitted into the original framework.

The final impression is of minimal change but the barn had first to be saved from literally tumbling down the hill. The whole roof structure was tilted with one gable end bulging three metres out of line and the other propped up by stone buttresses. Both gable ends were rebuilt and, having been stripped to expose damaged oak beams and rafters, the old pantiles were relaid and edged with three courses of stone around the eaves to give a traditional overhang. (The original thatch or stone had been replaced by pantiles at the turn of the century.) Where needed the walls were patched. They still lean slightly but are structurally sound. 'Richard has great faith that if a building has stood up for this long, there is no reason why it should not continue to do so,' says Tish loyally. And Richard agrees; 'You can worry too much. Admittedly the foundations were inadequate but I felt with three foot walls there was no need for underpinning.' Fortunately, the building engineer shared his view. After preliminary excavations, the ground level was raised to make room for drains and an under-floor heating system. As a back up, all the inside walls were sealed with an expanding polyurethane spray. Its phenomenal insulation properties mean the heating is seldom needed, especially as the central area is warmed by a large south-facing window fitted into the roof.

The barn follows the slope of the hill, stepping down from

Changes to the barn structure have been minimal: the layout fitted into the original framework, putting a sitting room in the hayloft, a kitchen in the stables below and a dining hall in the centre of the barn

the cobbled animal pen towards the stables. The natural incline is accentuated by the barn's four different levels that belie its 100-foot length. Standing in the dining hall you can look one way to a bedroom, another to the sitting room, which used to be the hayloft and, below, you can glimpse the kitchen. This ability to view the barn from different angles gives an added dimension to its perspective and volume. Although the living areas are all on different levels they have a continuity, linked by their overhead pattern of rafters. 'The roof structure was one of the nicest parts of the barn,' says Tish. 'We wanted to keep it there without accentuating it too much.' Plywood boarding between the rafters has been coloured with a soft-grey stain, rather than

Jamie and Fergus Fielden have tent-shaped bedrooms tucked in the eaves of the barn. A split-level floor increases their play area and provides more adventurous sleeping places.

look across to the master bedroom with its cantilevered floor that appears to float in space. An internal window casts extra light into the bedroom and increases the open-plan effect. And in the bathroom, part of the master bedroom, another window provides a vantage point for looking down on family life. From the main bedroom there are steps up to a children's bathroom and three tent-like rooms. 'We did feel a bit mean on bedroom size but wanted to keep the main space as uninterrupted as possible,' says Tish. She is a psychotherapist and likes children to be inventive with their own environment. Jamie and Fergus, aged nine and seven, have split-level bedrooms like adventure playgrounds where as an alternative to beds they nest in cupboards, shelves or boxes. Their

white paint, which gives a restful, uncontrived effect. It tones with the rough cut Dorset penants on the ground floor, chosen for practical and visual reasons. 'They suit our outdoor life with young children, animals and muddy gumboots tramping through the barn,' says Tish.

Steps from the dining hall lead up to the sitting room, partitioned from mid-air by a glass balcony. Raising two central roof trusses opened up the room into a tall apparently floating space. It has an informal atmosphere, furnished with fabric-draped sofas, cushioned wicker chairs, curtains sewn from striped Indian bedspreads and a child-resistant grey cord carpet that reflects the roof colouring. There are no sharp corners or edges to the solid white walls, studded with square ventilation holes that double as alcoves. From the glass balcony you

younger sister Rowan is tucked into a cosy bedroom halfway up the stairs.

The kitchen in the stables is surprisingly unrustic. 'We did have a tasteful wooden kitchen in our last barn but decided to be a bit different here with something practical and reasonably cheap,' explains Tish. As the family were desperate to move out of their mobile home, the kitchen was needed in a hurry. Richard decided to build units in M.D.F. (medium density fibre) – a material like thick, concentrated cardboard that can be shaped and chamfered to size. They were coated with turquoise Hammerite - a tough metallic paint with a silvery space-age look that contrasts with the oak ceiling joists and the rough timber post propped on a stone plinth. But the most dominant feature is the view through the large kitchen window across fields to the city of Bath; it is a great education in transport systems, watching the roads, railway, river and canal that move in parallel lines across the valley. The kitchen extends into an informal eating and television area, divided from cooking and practical quarters by open shelves and a wooden partition painted in stripes of seaside pink, cream and sky blue.

At the far end of the barn, beyond the dining hall, which is furnished with a green oak table, Wendy House, piano and billiards table, you come to a children's small sitting room converted from the cowshed. Further on, a dark cobbled workshop is shared between Tish's pottery, Richard's tools and an occasional horse. After four years the green oak woodwork, much of which was constructed by Richard, has shrunk and warped rather more than expected, giving the doors and dining table a rough homespun quality. 'I was slightly cavalier about the joinery, using unseasoned boards for the doors. It's the sort of thing you do in your own house but not for a client,' he adds.

The Fieldens bought four acres of land below the barn for their livestock, a family of horses, cows, sheep, pigs and goats that graze on fields sloping down to the river. Behind the barn, an orchard and vegetable garden have been planted on terraces levelled with building rubble. Tish has created a flower garden in what was a great dip, evened out by Richard's digger work. The soil is still stony but fertilized by years of cow dung. Her

original idea to grow only indigenous plants has broadened. 'To start with I really didn't want it to look suburban, or even allow myself a washing line!' So she filled the herbaceous border with old-fashioned perennials.

As an afterthought, the Fieldens restored the most derelict outhouse, a square stone forge built at the same time as the barn. It had served more recently as a chicken house where such diverse relics as a pair of old bellows, harnesses and nesting boxes were found rotting amongst trees that pushed through the roof. Now the exterior has been traditionally rebuilt with pegged, green oak boarding below a pantiled pyramid roof. From outside it looks like an enduring garden shed but inside seems more like the Tardis. Fitted into an uncompromising two-storey space there is a self-contained flat with kitchen, shower room, sitting room, and sleeping loft for children. The greatest surprise is an indoor swimming pool slotted into what was 'a dingy hole with four foot of headroom at one end'. It opens out into a conservatory that fills the double height of the building. Glass doors in the end wall open on to the garden, giving the pool an outdoor aspect on warm sunny days. Without wanting to sound ungrateful, Tish mentions that the only failing in her 'dream come true' is that her seedlings bolt too fast in the conservatory's warmth. Perhaps an out-of-sight cold frame is the last step to perfect happiness.

FIELD BARN

JEREMY AND PATRICIA BENSON

~

As Jeremy Benson sat on a bale of straw waiting for a partridge to drop out of the sky he noticed a large stone barn across the field. With its roof off and rafters rotting, it reminded him of a hunted elephant lying ungainly on its back. He had known the barn as a child when he lived close by in Gloucestershire. It had been in working use until the 1950s, part of a substantial group of eighteenth-century buildings where animals could shelter from the fierce Cotswold winters. When local agriculture changed from stock rearing to arable, the stone barn, cowhouse, manger and granary were abandoned. Slates were stripped from the barn to patch the village church roof in 1955, exposing its interior to the elements.

Jeremy Benson and his wife Patricia, both architects of historic buildings, were drawn to the neglected stone settlement. In the following spring of 1964, they rented a primitive shepherd's cottage beside the barn. After making the cottage habitable they spent two years contemplating the barn, which by now had collapsed still further. Yet its derelict state fired their architects' imagination and, after negotiating a sale, they were given permission to convert the barn into a house.

As Vice-Chairman of the Society for the Protection of Ancient Buildings for the last 16 years, Jeremy Benson has ambivalent feelings about living in a barn. His own rebuilding work was a *fait accompli* when the Society announced its disapproval of domestic conversions. But the Bensons' barn proves how a redundant building can work as a house and still enhance the landscape. Jeremy Benson is concerned by the number of old buildings passing rapidly out of agricultural use. 'Of course agriculture is the best answer for derelict farm buildings but you can't expect farmers to go on using barns that don't fit their machinery. In a village pressure to turn barns into houses is difficult to resist. The ones out in the landscape are more important because they are not hidden by other buildings.' His own barn stands prominently in an arable setting, surrounded by rolling corn fields and woodland. 'Without this barn the ground wouldn't compose. Leaving a building in it adds importance to the landscape – they both benefit from each other's presence.'

The renovated stone barn and exquisite English country garden are a far cry from the sad buildings that were once grouped around the farmyard. According to scratchings on the stone wall, the barn was built in 1746 for storing and threshing grain, which was beaten by hand using flails on a wooden floor in the central bay. (Stone floors came after the invention of threshing machines in 1786.) Each end of the barn was paved with red bricks where mangel-wurzels were stored. In the galleries above, sheaves of corn waited for threshing.

Regardless of their five children the Bensons kept the barn as one open space: a 60-foot living room with a small sitting room and kitchen at either end; a bedroom and multi-purpose office-cum-store in the galleries. All other bedrooms and bathrooms are squeezed into the refurbished cottage. Now that Jeremy and Patricia are grandparents they can enjoy their children and grandchildren under separate roofs.

During the barn conversion they considered turning a stone manger into a row of extra bedrooms but it came down in the end, leaving a curved stone backdrop to a prolific herbaceous border. Two remaining walls of a large cowhouse shelter the far side of the garden, grandified by stone copings laid along the top. The barred window of the cowhouse has been kept but moved to the centre of the wall.

The Bensons' preoccupation with symmetry is obvious. The balanced garden, walls, borders and central steps from barn to lawn have a formality that is curiously sympathetic to the manicured fields beyond. 'As architects we like to have plenty of lines, levels and form,' says Jeremy. To add form to the plain rectangular building, they reinstated a midstrey in the centre of the barn – the original cart entrance that jutted out into the farmyard. The restored midstrey is a gabled wood and glass projection that opens on to a terrace, uniting both barn and garden. Its expanse of glass is balanced by four columns of large-paned windows spaced across the stone façade. The lower openings are all French windows that lead on to a wide terrace that surrounds the barn. This continuity between barn and garden is emphasized by an overlap in materials. The Cotswold stone walls are the same inside and out; the internal brick floor extends over the terrace and wide garden steps. There is a calm, undecorated quality about it that reflects a low-maintenance approach adopted 20 years ago.

Having rebuilt the barn with enduring materials, the Bensons tried to do the minimum to its structure. Aware of probable damp they left the stone walls unplastered, Jeremy regrets the small damp proof course in one area, realizing it has caused a weakness in the massive wall. 'With a large building, the wind blows and forces it to move around a little – it's the damp course that's the line of movement,' he explains. The barn was reroofed with old stone slates (which cost £4,000 in 1969) laid over a new oak frame and rafters with insulation sandwiched between. To add headroom in the galleries, the tie beams and roof trusses were raised, increasing the height from six to seven foot six. Extra inches were gained by laying a beam and plank floor which gives a more solid tread but less depth than a standard beam and joist floor. Most of the woodwork in the barn is oak but chestnut was used for the outside joinery, doors and window frames. Although it looks like oak, it is stronger, takes preservative and weathers to a silvery grey.

Paintwork is minimal; outside, only the large iron gutters and downpipes have been painted using camouflage green. Inside, two tall free-standing chimneys are painted white in contrast to the stone walls and warm red bricks. Inspiration for the floor came from the surviving bricked areas in the barn. Only a few could be salvaged to edge flower beds, so new pavior bricks were laid inside and out. On the terrace their surface has been smoothed by a terrazzo grinder which gives a worn, weathered look. Inside, polish was applied over a ground surface – a tortuous process which involved grinding the floor twice. The first coat of polish was too hard and turned the floor white with scratches. The only way to remove it was to sandblast the floor, regrind, then apply a different polish. Unfortunately, by this second time, the roof was on and the Bensons had moved in.

Although one uninterrupted space, the barn is large enough to fulfil several functions at once – combining as playroom,

A clipped box poodle stands among the alchemilla in the Bensons' vegetable garden next to the shepherd's cottage. Artichokes, sweet peas, beans and lettuces grow here, sheltered by stone walls.

dining room, drawing room and office. 'It's marvellous,' enthuses Patricia, 'there is enough space for lots of people to do their own thing at the same time.' The barn was deliberately under-furnished 20 years ago; 'It was lovely, smooth and empty – it's extraordinary how it's filled up,' she remarks. Despite the accumulation of sofas, tables and plants, the soaring height of the central bays supplies an extravagant feeling of space. The airiness is emphasized by bare windows, a decision made after calculating that it would take 286 yards of fabric to make curtains for them. Nine paper lanterns hang from the beams, like white balloons, which were chosen after looking at the price of more traditional light fittings.

The furniture arrangement changes with the seasons. In summer when the midstrey becomes a conservatory-style sitting room, the rocking chair and sofas are moved away from the fireplace towards the garden. Three long ash tables (the first bought from Conran, two more copied by a local carpenter) are also movable elements. One is usually spread with a jigsaw puzzle in winter, another buried under architectural plans. Joined lengthways, they seat at least thirty for family parties. Besides a kitchen, the Bensons wanted one enclosed room that would feel cosy on winter evenings and be an easy size to heat. The result is a small booklined sitting room at the end of the barn with a tall west-facing window to catch the evening sun. It cried out for an open hearth but there was no question of installing a third chimney. Instead Jeremy devised a dual re-

volving fireplace that rotates from the barn to parlour. It means
you can take your drink and the fire with you into the next
room. Both fireplaces are identical with a pale Guiting stone
surround, a Berlin-black canopy and lime mortared fireback.

The kitchen reflects the Bensons' practical nature, precision
planned with oak cupboards, shelves, counter, kitchen table
and tiny built-in larder, all fitted logically into the brick-floored
room. Like the parlour, it is a separate part of the barn but its
decoration and character reflect the whole scheme. French
windows open from the kitchen on to a dining terrace shaded
by a sailcloth awning and rampant clematis strung from a flat-
roofed pergola.

Jeremy and Patricia's bedroom is reached by open oak stairs
which lead up from the main barn space. With a wooden floor,
rough stone walls, pine chests and cream cotton bedspread, it
has a rustic calm, dominated by views from three uncurtained
windows. One looks beyond the shepherd's cottage to an immaculate vegetable garden where artichokes, sweet peas, beans
and lettuces grow between stone walls and clipped box topiary.
The other window faces south overlooking the flower garden
where families of rock roses, alliums, euphorbias and irises spill
from herbaceous borders. Perhaps the most aesthetic surprise
of all is a discreet swimming pool sheltered by the cowhouse
walls. It looks like an ornamental pond edged with terracotta
urns until you notice its depth and water temperature. There is
no glittering blue and white to catch the eye: avoiding a clash
between man and landscape, the pool has been painted a
muted sea-green and the concrete pavings around the water
suitably distressed to an ancient patina.

*Even after 25 years the barn appears refreshingly uncluttered and
orderly. The sofa and chairs are arranged for winter close to the re-
volving fireplace. In the gallery above, copies of* Country Life *are
stacked beside seeds harvested from the garden.*

LOWER HOUSE FARM

PENNY AND ROBIN OLIVER

～

Fine Georgian farmhouse, pity about the barn, was the verdict when Robin and Penny Oliver moved to the Welsh borders 15 years ago. With their house, outbuildings and 13 acres came a derelict timber-framed barn, 60 foot long with a gaping tin roof and ramshackle, cladded walls. Its exact age and history were uncertain but two A-shaped cruck frames suggested sixteenth-century origins, extended to five bays in the early eighteenth century. Once a threshing barn, it was also used for housing grain, animals, straw and chickens – still in occupance when the Olivers first arrived.

At first they spent part of their time in London and so were not faced with the permanent barn dilemma. It remained in a state of collapse for two years until Robin inherited a grand piano from his father which forced them to make a decision. As there was not enough room in the farmhouse for a piano, the obvious answer was to take on the barn. It was an awesome task that meant complete rebuilding, although financial and structural limits made it impossible to keep the full length of the barn. It was too large and too dilapidated; the timber frame dangled from the roof, touching ground level in only three places. How it remained standing at all was a mystery to the timber-frame expert from the Council.

The transformation from wreck to inhabitable barn took seven years, several of which were spent waiting for the appropriate people. An archi-

tect was recommended through advice from the Society for the Protection of Ancient Buildings, but then the Olivers had a two year wait for the builders. They had put the job out to tender and chose a local Malvern based company who, despite inexperience, accepted the challenge of dismantling the barn, mending the timber frame, then replacing it with oak pegs between the new roof, walls and floor. Luckily both parties had faith in each other. When the job was finished, the builders, barn experts by then, admitted that they had only agreed to the scheme because Penny seemed so sure it could be done. Unknown to them, she had been carried along by their enthusiasm.

Permission was given by the Council which was in favour of restoration, providing the cruck frames were kept. 'They accepted the fact that the barn had to be smaller,' explains Penny. 'We could only afford to keep three of the bays, so we slid two together and took out the threshing floor.' As well as changing size, the barn changed direction. Instead of standing end on, it is now parallel to the road looking into the garden at right angles to the house. 'We face rather curiously north-west, on the setting line of the winter sun. On the shortest day the sun goes down directly level with the end window,' says Penny. By moving the barn, the Olivers found it qualified as a new building, exempt from VAT on building bills. 'We wanted to change its position

RIGHT, A pear tree mural – symbolizing Penny and Robin's five-acre orchard – decorates three panels above an architrave of shelves, which have been pegged into recesses between the wall posts

BELOW, The timber frame structure of the derelict, collapsing barn was re-assembled between a new roof, walls and floor – an exacting seven-year process

and that financial advantage tipped the balance.'

Compared to most of the later progress, dismantling the barn was a surprisingly rapid operation. Penny returned from a day away to find it in pieces on the ground. 'It really did look just like a heap of firewood – in fact the builders had been offered £25 for the lorry load of ancient oak beams'. Once the barn had been levered down and crowbarred apart, the slowest task was prising the cladding and rusty corrugated iron from the timber framework. All the essential pieces were loaded on to a lorry and taken off to the builders' yard. The structure was away for a year being mended and then reassembled to match the architect's model. The plan to recreate its original haphazard outline had to be modified by the builders. Although they appreciated the idea, it was awkward to produce something non-symmetrical from scratch.

Inside, the plan was to keep two of the bays as an open space with a raised gallery floor and study below, fitted between the cruck frames at the oldest end of the barn. It repeats the original layout of a loft floor at one end of the building, where candle burns on the beams suggest that there had been occasional human habitation. For the Olivers the barn is an extension of the farmhouse; a sitting room, workplace, somewhere to entertain and sometimes sleep when the house is full. After two years of 'unhurriable' building work, it was ready on 23 December, in time to celebrate Christmas with 17 relations. By then the ceremonial fir tree growing in the garden had overshot the 21-foot ground to ridge height and had to be pruned to fit. A large star strung from the beams still hangs as a permanent reminder of the Olivers' first Christmas in the barn.

The internal framework is as authentic as possible. Apart from the windows inserted between panels, the arrangement of timbers in the walls and roof trusses follows the original layout. The differences lie in the new structure. Rebuilding on a fresh site meant that every aspect of the barn could be insulated. Before the finished frames were fitted back into place, what looked like a swimming pool had been dug for the underfloor heating, sandwiched between a foot of insulation and concrete. It is extremely eco-nomical especially when helped by cunning roof and wall insulation, and also eliminates radiators which would look incongruous in a barn. Penny realized the cold factor of exposing timber framework on both sides of a building; 'You are bound to be cold unless you conceal the frame on one side.' The new walls are deceptively thick. Elm cladding, cut from a stricken wood in Gloucestershire, is nailed over insulated matting to a new timber frame. Inside, plaster set into the original timber panels conceals a layer of insulating styrofoam. As elm tends to twist with age, it leaves inviting gaps in the cladding for intruders. So to protect against birds and insects burrowing in the insulation, the whole barn has been wrapped with a fine wire mesh, like a hair net. In summer the creak of twisting elm – 'a quite startling bang, crunch, crack' – adds to the birdsong.

The interior has a rustic atmosphere accentuated by panels of oak cleaving fitted between the wall studs at ground and gallery level. A few tattered remnants of cleaving left in the original barn were beyond repair so the chief carpenters, John Young and Geoff Wood, learnt to weave strips of green oak at Avoncroft museum in Bromsgrove. Two oak trees later they had mastered the craft; hacking the upright trunk into triangles, drawing a 'fro' up the grain to slice the oak into pliable strips, then weaving with brute force between the uprights. 'It did take a surprising amount of oak – and there were a few disasters,' recalls Penny. But fortunately the offcuts kept the Olivers supplied with kindling wood for quite some time.

A generous quantity of light floods into the barn through different sized windows which were inserted at random between the panels. As they are mounted on the cladding no frames are visible from inside which gives the impression of empty panels rather than windows. The effect is emphasized by a lack of curtains. Instead there are movable elm frames stapled with fine matting and crimson felt that cover the windows at night. Most daylight comes through massive French windows in the middle bay – an enlargement of the original cart doors. The new glass doors are screened by elm shutters that merge into the cladded exterior walls.

Draughtproof glazing on

The scale of the grand piano is matched by an accumulation of large country furniture and Oriental rugs and kilims that complement the warm burnished colours of the barn interior

windows and doors, combined with the insulation and under-floor heating, keep a constant temperature for the grand piano and ancestral oil paintings on the walls. Except in mid-winter there is little need for the two woodburning stoves installed in the gallery and stud below. 'We thought the barn would be much colder but it is like one big storage heater, running on Economy Seven electricity. In four months its heating costs are less than one room in the farmhouse,' says Penny. All the electrical sockets are fitted into the wooden sole plate which juts out like a solid skirting board. Electrical wiring wanders discreetly across the roof trusses, hidden from sight wherever possible. A strong tungsten halogen light fixed to the horizontal collar beam lights the central area, backed by downlighters. On the gallery floor there are spotlights at ground level which create a rather theatrical effect after dark.

Decoration has been kept to burnished Tuscan colours – applied with a primitive touch – echoing what could have been found 300 years ago. After experimenting with different effects and combinations, ground pigments of yellow ochre and Van Dyke brown from Cornelissen, a specialist paint shop in Covent Garden, London, were mixed with limewash to coat the rough plastered panels. 'Slaking the limewash is quite frightening. It comes up hissing and spitting out of a tin bucket!' After a coat of white limewash, followed by yellow ochre, Penny stabbed a brew of Van Dyke brown over the top. Its warm textural effect is echoed in the Vietnamese seagrass matting laid over the concrete floor. All the materials and colours in the barn are natural; nothing plastic except the temporary intrusion of Penny's computer. It is a perfect setting for the Olivers' Oriental rugs and kilims, whose burnt earth tones and geometric designs reflect the colour and form of the interior. They hang beside paintings, cover the floor or drape from the elm banisters – where the foot of each post is carved

into a blunted point as if reflecting the kilim's weave.

The sitting room on the gallery floor has a secluded feeling, detached from the open area below. A central staircase leads up to a calm, comfortable space with ochre limewashed walls, elm floorboards laid with rugs, a cream damask wing-chair beside the stove and terracotta linen sofas ranged against cleft oak walls. Etruscan reds recur on both levels of the barn, colouring wall panels, bookbindings, tapestried seats and a background to an architrave of shelves around the front door which have been pegged into recesses between the wall posts. Three panels above the shelves are decorated with a delicate mural of pears and blossom; its faded quality giving a worn, age-old impression that captures the stiff blossom and angular branches of Herefordshire pear trees – symbolic of the Olivers' five-acre orchard, harvested each autumn for perry and cider.

Furniture throughout the barn is robust and old country; 'Anything small looks lost in this setting . . . also I would rather have much less in here,' remarks Penny about a glut of inherited furniture. The collection of tapestried chairs, oak chests, side tables, books and *objets trouvés* from travels with the Foreign Office create still life tableaux, lit by shafts of sunlight that slant across the barn.

Below the sitting room gallery is Robin's study; a book-lined enclave, more gentleman's den than barn, where he tucks himself away with a library of music and books. Upstairs Penny works at her desk, helping protect woodland for the Council for the Protection of Rural England. In summer she sits with the giant glass doors thrown open on to a stone terrace made from the old threshing floor.

After so long in production the finished barn is a great reward. 'It was a full-time task that I wouldn't like to have done in a hurry,' she reflects. 'Although, having learnt so much the first time, I could definitely do it again much more quickly'.

STANSBACH BARN

CHARLES JANSON

~

There is enough room in Charles Janson's barn for his three disparate occupations. His stained glass features on a modest number of windows and lampshades, but there is also ample space to decorate panels, doors and windows in a cowshed that adjoins the barn. The studio is shared by two flight simulators, like booths from an amusement arcade where Charles practises a quick screen take-off between designs. Further on, occupying a large share of the barn, the stage is set for a jamming session with instruments and sound equipment ready for band practice. Charles on bass guitar is a founder member of Two Left Feet, a name that has changed as often as the line-up that has played the Welsh marches and beyond for the last 14 years. Such alternative pursuits contrast with the pastoral calm of Offa's Dyke and the Black Mountains – but this stretch of the Herefordshire border country near Presteigne and Hay-on-Wye is an established refuge for artists, musicians and writers.

Stansbach Barn dominates a group of early-Victorian farm buildings, erected in 1840 at the height of agricultural expansion; a slate-roofed threshing barn with a stone base and timber framework above adjoin a long low cowshed and bull pen. Once the farm they served had been sold, the redundant buildings were left to deteriorate for nine years until Charles bought them. Although they came with outline planning permission, Charles discarded the accompanying design for an eight-roomed dwelling that totally ignored the character and scale of the barn. 'It was awful, far too twee and dinkified,' laughs Charles, 'so we decided to change it all completely.'

His layout was for a basic two-up, two-down with a central hall and staircase rising through the 55-foot barn. It may now be a house but it is not remotely domesticated. Although the interior has been partitioned into vast rooms and a first floor expanded from the original granary, its simplicity gives an impression of reluctant change. Charles's approach was to match the robust scale of the barn's structure by keeping its generous proportions and solid oak timbers. Once the plans had been approved, Charles recruited a team of five local friends, each one an expert in plumbing, wiring, carpentry, roofing and brickwork and appointed himself general dogsbody and tea maker.

The barn was in a terrible condition, leaning alarmingly to one side. Charles's team worked for eight months through the wet spring and summer of 1983, stripping the barn to a roofless skeleton while shaky parts were underpinned and foundations dug for a chimney and internal walls. Endless rain filled the trenches, so rather than constantly baling out, they worked underwater for part of the time. Such radical rebuilding made it possible to change the barn's shape from a rectangle to an E-shape without the middle prong. Now it has a rather colonial aspect with a veranda and first-floor balcony filling a recess cut out of the original façade. 'There were no nice turns or interesting corners and I wanted to add some character to the building,' explains Charles. The veranda, paved with flagstones from the old

As the barn needed radical rebuilding, Charles was able to cut into the façade to make a first-floor balcony and colonial veranda, paved with flagstones taken from the threshing floor

threshing floor, makes an alfresco sitting room, decorated with clematis and roses. Upstairs, a rampant wisteria frames a view from the balcony to the Black Mountains.

As the only openings in the original structure were cart doors on each side of the barn, 32 windows of various sizes were fitted into the new layout. The frames and two new doors were all made from an oak tree that Charles bought which had been planted in 1897 to commemorate Queen Victoria's diamond jubilee. The tree was well seasoned but for the new beams and three replacement tie-beams Charles used green oak. Other materials came from dismantled houses; the pitch-pine doors and maple floor boards for the upstairs rooms came from Yorkshire. 'Everything seemed to fall into place,' recalls Charles. 'There were no awful hassles but I can still remember it driving me crazy.' Although far from conventional, the barn has all the practical assets of a modern house. Gas central heating is backed up by styrofoam insulation in the timber framework, fixed between the external rendering and plaster inside. Downstairs in the music room, the walls are soundproofed to muffle the sounds of band practices.

Charles's kitchen is the main living room. It is the most decorated, furnished part of the barn, reminiscent of a remote French farmhouse. The scorched harvest colours – straw, Burnt Siena, terracotta – on the walls, floors and furniture give a settled feel that belie its modernity. The walls have a time-worn look, created by an ochre glaze over eggshell paint, sealed with varnish. A quarry-tiled floor in harvest gold and rust-red unites the colours of the room, laid by Charles himself in a diamond pattern with a square border. To comply with building regulations it sits over a deep layer of rubble, piled up to raise the kitchen floor level with the road. During the conversion, Charles's kitchen became the local tip where neighbours were encouraged to dump rock and debris as ballast.

The room is furnished with large simple pieces typical of uncluttered male taste; a wooden pub bench beside a massive oak table; a bulky 1950s radiogram picked up for £3 in a local sale and an eccentric oak cupboard of similar origin. For lounging around, there is a bat-

After removing a partition wall in the granary, Charles kept the vast space for his bedroom, exaggerating its size with a puritan amount of furniture. The previous occupants were pet foxes.

tered camel-back sofa which is ranged against three large windows that open into the garden – once the farmyard, now turfed with grass. Domestic elements are minimal; a traditional cream Aga hung with cast-iron woks and pans and a double sink set into a wooden worksurface.

The kitchen leads into a square, wooden-floored hall where one of the original openings is now filled by substantial doors on to a veranda. They are flanked by blue and red stained-glass windows with a simple diamond pattern repeated on Tiffany-style lampshades, one overhead, the other on Charles's desk tucked against the wall. The desk, inherited from his grandmother, is an old oak serving table with handsome rectangular legs and has been copied on a larger scale for the kitchen. A curved oak staircase leads from the hall up to the balcony where Charles sits in the early evening plotting a route for his next microlight jaunt. French windows lead on to the balcony, accentuating the barn's bohemian aspect, curtained with precious Afghan kilims. 'I used to collect them in the sixties when they were two a penny,' muses Charles.

The vastness of his bedroom is exaggerated by its sparse furniture; just a brass bed, the odd chair, tall thin cupboard, kilims scattered over maple floorboards and skimpy red toile curtains. It occupies the granary which was divided in two by the last eccentric farmer, George Price, who kept grain in one half and pet foxes in the other. The second bedroom across the landing has similar proportions, well lit by four windows with inspirational views. It is now the spare room again after use as a studio by a Dutch artist Katrin Poelsma whose landscapes decorate the walls. Charles likes the barn to be used as a work place as well as somewhere to live. 'Barn conversions don't feel like proper houses – they need people in them with occupations,' he says. It is open house to his family and friends who come and go at weekends.

From upstairs you look down on the cowshed and bull pen which extend at right angles from the barn to form an L-shape around the old farmyard. After replacing acres of slate on the long cowshed roof, fitting windows into the stone walls and laying a concrete floor, it made

The kitchen is the heart of the barn, used more for living in than domestic pursuits. From here Charles can keep an eye on his Bristol motor car parked below a red brick granary.

a basic studio, large enough to work on commissions for stained-glass doors and windows. There are plans one day to turn the bull pen beyond into a conservatory, replacing its slate roof with glass. A more imminent step is to restore a detached granary that faces the gable end of the barn. So far it has been a useful workshop where Charles built himself a glider, but the first floor space has great potential for a compact studio or granny flat.

Lodged below the red-brick granary are three important possessions; Charles's Bristol motorcar, in fine running order; a painted gypsy caravan, 'home for a year', and a prized 1958 tractor bought cheaply at a farm sale on a lucky day when no one else was bidding. He has loyal respect for this old friend. 'We couldn't have built the place without it – a great workhorse that lifted load after load.'

PARK HOUSE

IAN AND RIKE LANDON

—~—

From outside the only sign of human habitation is a low chimney and two downpipes against the barn walls. There are no openings in the kirkstone slate walls, just impenetrable-looking cart doors firmly barred against hikers sheltering in the hay. The buildings stand down a secluded track in the Lake District, a tall craggy barn towering over two white cottages that conjure pictures of a busy Mrs Tiggywinkle inside.

It was during a holiday spent in one of the cottages that Ian and Rike Landon set their hearts on their future home. Although the barn and surrounding land were let to a farmer, an old lady who occupied the other cottage had assumed command of the whole settlement – she had after all lived there for 25 years. So the Landons' plan to buy and convert the barn needed tact and patience. It took over two years for, although the farmer agreed to move out, the old lady remained firmly ensconced until she died. Added to this was a battle for planning permission. As the barn stood on Lake District parkland it came under strict planning control. Conversions are rarely allowed unless a barn adjoins an 'inhabitable dwelling', preferably with a connecting door between. Despite the old lady's occupancy, Ian Landon persisted and discovered a vital link from the barn to cottage – a blocked doorway hidden behind an oak lintel and lime mortar that fulfilled the requirement to extend into the barn.

The change from nineteenth-century barn to domestic retreat is deliberately discreet. The combined priorities of privacy and respect for the original structure have made an individual home and studio. Ian Landon is an artist who includes building as part of his art. The barn – rather like an 'enormous stone sculpture' - took three years of his time. 'After all, the art is in the doing,' he believes. This is his seventh and final project. Its predecessors have all been agricultural buildings in England, Germany and Italy. It is their sense of antiquity, their indigenous materials and vernacular style, simple enough for a layman to follow, that inspire him. Past projects gave him enough expertise to plot every stage of the barn's restoration. Working single-handed up to the plaster-board stage, he rebuilt walls, chimneys, fitted windows, laid floors, plumbing, electricity and re-slated the roof. When Ian began, the barn was dark and derelict, lit only by tall cart doors set high in the wall. They opened below the protruding roofline, into a soaring first-floor space. Having been built as a Lakeland or 'broach' barn, there is a stone ramp up to the doors where carts and wagons would unload. Now the slope of boulders, hauled from the river bed, is carpeted in moss and foxgloves and shields a box-edged herb garden that has replaced the wilderness in front of the barn.

At ground level, where once there were two dank slate-panelled stables fitted with rotting oak stalls, there are now the kitchen and dining room which connect with the restored cottage. Stairs from ground level lead up to the barn studio and living room which has a small study enclosed at one side. Above this Ian installed a gallery floor with a bal-

From a distance the tall barn with a steep slate roof shows no sign of human habitation. Moving closer, the only hint is a low chimney and two downpipes against the windowless walls.

cony and bedroom beyond. The main living space has a calm, cool atmosphere created by light from a north-facing window. For art's sake Ian kept the south front unbroken. 'I wanted cool, blue light to work by, not yellow sunlight,' so the front of the barn remains a solid wall of uneven slates pegged together with giant 'through-stones' – 'like a huge lego set with complications'. Outside, the drab olive cart doors blend against the greeny-grey wall. From inside they are invisible, screened by a

ABOVE, *A glass cabinet in a corner of the barn brims with still-life inspiration*

RIGHT, *Creative art takes priority in the barn, lit by a large, north-facing window cut out of an end wall. Glass doors lead into a cosier study filled with books, paintings and a grand piano*

plasterboard wall. A small entrance cut into this wall behind
one cart door opens with Lilli-
putian effect on to a pastoral
landscape.

Typical of a Lakeland barn, the high cart doors opened
onto a ramp where wagons would unload. There is still a
discreet entrance at this level.

studio window and then rebuilt
to match the original stonework. Dark-brown painted
frames merge into the wall,
making the windows undetectable from a distance. Their
rough slate sills jut out, acting as a balance to the protruding
'through-stones'. Around the openings, the stone slates are set
in place with sculpted green cement. Elsewhere a characteristic

One of the most exacting tasks was knocking holes in the
walls for nine windows of different sizes and shapes. Much of
the gable end wall had to be dismantled for the eight-foot

lack of pointing continues. The largest cracks are filled with loose lime mortar which proved an open invitation to a maternity ward of nesting birds who settled in the gaps.

Establishing the ground level was a crucial stage. As the floor was damp and sloping without proper foundations, the only way to eliminate the water seeping into the walls and floor was to dig over two foot down to the pinnel, a layer of clay and gravel, that gave a rock-like base to build on. Following traditional methods, the materials were then layered, first with massive boulders wedged between earth and sand which formed the foundations below a PVC screen, acting as a damp course that carried on up the walls. The final layer was six inches of concrete. Putting a proper damp course into the large bouldered walls was impossible. The alternative was to inject a silicone substance into both sides of the walls, making them impermeable to wind and rain. 'It's endless problem-solving from the minute you start, an approach that has a crazy level of dedication. It's not something I'd advise a best friend to do,' admits Ian.

The interior reflects the Landons' taste for mixing old with new. A giant silver chimney flue shines against the rough stone wall, towering from a woodburning stove. Angular wooden armchairs are grouped around the fireplace, ready for conversation, but the surrounding space is arranged for creative work. Easels, drawing boards, print chests and glass cabinets filled with still-life inspiration stand on pale blue-grey linoleum – chosen to enhance the northern light. White walls, roof and balcony brighten the barn and emphasize its spaciousness. The dark roof trusses, beams and ceiling joists stand out in contrast; a monochrome effect sharpened by landscape paintings and art posters that draw the eye upward. The roof has an equal

simplicity, with a pitched white slope striped by purlins. Wherever possible the original timbers have been retained, inlaid between the layers of insulation and plasterboard. Any rotten parts were replaced with timbers bought from a local farmer.

Glass doors open from the main barn space into a small white study that doubles as a sitting room and occasional spare bedroom. A grand piano occupies much of the floor, and wall space is shared by paintings and books stacked on simple shelves. Stairs in a corner of the barn lead down to the kitchen and dining room where windows have transformed the stables into cosy low-ceilinged rooms. The kitchen is rustic but well organized. Microwave, storage jars, toaster, olive oil flagons crowd on to pine ledges against the wall. Cooking equipment hangs from the beams, beside pans, ladles, sieves and garlic hooked on to a pergola-like rack across the ceiling. Culinary arts are watched by Botticelli's *Primavera* maidens, a print of which hangs above the kitchen table.

The lean-to cowshed that stood against the stable wall was knocked through to create a back porch; its door reached by slate steps made from panels in the old stables. Land behind the barn slopes steeply into a terraced garden of stone walls, narrow lawns and flower beds – cultivated by Rike. It is shaded by a towering chestnut, declared dangerous by a tree surgeon who cut 30 foot from its spire.

The final remaining phase is to tackle a derelict pigsty rotting at the bottom of the garden. Ian plans to replace the tattered slate roof with glass, lay a floor over the mud ground and make himself a print workshop. After that, he may finally relax – or at least pick up a paintbrush and transfer his creativity on to paper.

THE GRANARY

ALEXA QUEENSBERRY

~

Alexa Queensberry's barns punctuate an empty stretch of green Wiltshire landscapes. Visible for miles, they stand alone down a rutted farm track surrounded by a vast arable patchwork of land. Discovering the barns ended a four-year search for somewhere to live. It did not have to be a barn but it did have to be in Wiltshire where Alexa spent holidays and weekends from London with some if not all of her five children. While househunting, she lived locally in a rented cottage scanning the property pages of the *Salisbury Journal*. Then one week there it was, an indistinct photograph of a redundant farm settlement. Rushing to investigate, Alexa knew at once that she had found a home. Altogether it consisted of two crumbling stone cottages plus, a little way off, a barn with an adjoining granary. Alexa bought the lot. She restored the cottages, then sold them. The barn and granary she restored and converted into one large family house with a hall and vast drawing room in the hay barn, a giant kitchen, sitting room and bedrooms in the granary. It needed courage to take them on but from the start Alexa had no doubts. Nor any lack of im-

agination. 'I knew they would be absolutely marvellous,' she recalls with a quiet determination that masterminded all stages of the conversion.

The granary was Victorian, stone and red brick, in reasonable condition but needed drastic structural changes to make it habitable, divided as it was between shallow storeys connected by a ladder. The upper roof space, not intended for humans, was dissected by five impossibly low tie beams that meant constant ducking or living with permanent concussion. The only way to add height was by jacking up the whole building from below. Luckily the basic walls lent themselves to such Lego-style methods. Like a timber-framed building in reverse, the walls were cladded between brick posts which, after removing the roof slates, could be gradually chipped away to make space for a new layer of stone – a process that meant the ceilings on both floors could be raised, adding height and a grander perspective to the interior.

Lack of daylight was another problem, but more easily overcome. As the only openings were on one side of the granary,

Even at first sight (BELOW) *Alexa Queensberry could envisage the barn as a family house*

The red-brick granary (BELOW) *was in sound condition but needed a row of extra windows to let in more light*

three similar windows with matching red-brick surrounds were spaced along the opposite side. A glass panel set above the old stable door adds to the light in the six-windowed kitchen. The quantity of light became one of Alexa's chief preoccupations, 'I fretted terribly about not having enough windows, but the builders kept insisting it would be all right – and it is,' she says.

The barn and granary stand on a slope which exaggerates

The barn and granary stand on a slope which exaggerates their different heights and shapes. Once inside, the arrangement of light, airy spaces unites the two buildings

the different roof heights. Raising the granary closed the gap slightly, but the hay barn is still noticeably taller. Its collapse was averted by repairs to the brick-based timber walls, propped up for years by wooden buttresses. The hall now fills a gaping hole that tunnelled through the barn, framing the horizon like a viewfinder.

From the outside the buildings seem related more by proximity than any architectural similarity. Before the conversion

*The large flagstoned hall is flooded with light by windows
that reach from ground level to the rafters. An oak staircase
leads to the drawing room and on up to a
galleried landing*

their only link was through a door in the granary loft that dropped down into the barn below by means of a ladder. Now, from the inside, the only clue that two buildings have been united is the different floor levels that rise gradually from kitchen to drawing room. The central hall, spanning the full barn height, gives an immediate impression of light and space. From here an oak staircase leads to a galleried landing where, suspended between roof and ground, you absorb the different levels and sweeping view through windows on both sides. The best vantage point is the glass balcony that juts out above the front door giving a traditional overhang to the entrance and shelter from the fierce winds that scream across the treeless valley.

Alexa was tempted to continue the full barn height into the drawing room but knew such a vast area would be impossible to heat. Even with a lower ceiling there is still a sense of space and grand proportion augmented by a huge stone fireplace. Brilliant flashes of colour come from a delphinium-blue sofa scattered with bold silky cushions and a striking Regency couch upholstered in a fabric of cobalt-blue stripes. Daylight floods through four bare windows slotted behind the beams. A deep shelf cut out of the wall runs around the room like a high window seat where children like to perch. 'It's absolutely fine in here without curtains until darkest mid-winter when you can feel a bit like a goldfish,' says Alexa. 'I suppose I will find some material one day.' Inevitably when it is just family the Queensberrys use the small 'snug' next to the kitchen, but the drawing room is perfect for large parties. Over 170 guests came to Alexa's barn-warming; 'It was pouring with rain and even with lots of children it didn't feel too crushed.' The barn layout is ideal for entertaining. Alexa has visions of an elegant musical soirée with an audience in the drawing room and doors thrown open to a Beethoven string quartet on the landing above.

Upstairs in the bedrooms and bathrooms, there is more blue, but also Alexa's favourite ice-cream colours, vanilla, strawberry pink and pistachio. The boys occupy two connecting rooms which are fitted under the eaves above the drawing room and have a more neutral scheme; white walls between rough timbers, and limed-oaked shelving set into the wall. An original opening in the gable end became a window where Alexa's son, Milo, has a desk for homework. Back in the granary there are four bedrooms and two bathrooms on either side of a narrow passage. 'Somehow, one had to fit rooms into the empty spaces,' explains Alexa. The ceilings are low to accommodate water tanks and storage space above – except for Alexa's own bedroom. The far end of the granary is her domain. Her bedroom, not quite as large as the kitchen below, is tall and airy with windows that face east, west and south – a transformation from 'the big dark hole' it once was. The new windows lighten the pistachio-green walls and silver-grey tie beams which may look the colour of weathered oak, but are in fact painted to hide a disastrous coat of creosote that was slapped on by the builders when Alexa wasn't watching. The resulting colour has undone the horror and blends perfectly with the interior, reflecting the greyish-green in the stencilled curtains that hang from simple wooden poles. A high brass bed with an antique patchwork quilt dominates the room. Other furniture – a pine chest of

drawers, dressing table and day bed – are ranged around the wall, underlining the uncluttered atmosphere. Alexa's young daughter Beatrice has a replica bedroom in miniature, equally pistachio and pretty with stencilled furniture and curtains, and cotton durries laid over the matting. Next door to them both is a small, pale green bathroom with a cast-iron bath and cotton lace curtains.

Alexa has two theories about a kitchen; 'It either has to be so small and organized that you can stand in one place and reach everything, or a very large room that you can live in.' Her kitchen is definitely the living-in sort, large enough for two tables, a rocking horse, a desk and massive pine dresser bought cheaply in London because it was too big for most houses. The

Alexa's light, sunny bedroom is a transformation from the original cramped dark hole in the granary roof. The pale-green walls blend with the grey beams.

opposite wall is filled by a dark-green Aga set into a stone chimney breast that matches the drawing room fireplace. The kitchen dresser, cupboards, shelves and tables brim with china, books, photographs, toys and unpacked shopping. 'It could easily have extended the whole length of the granary, but such a big kitchen would have been ridiculous.' Instead there is a 'snug'; the Queensberry's informal sitting room furnished with comfortable sofas and armchairs gathered around an old pine fireplace. White walls are brightened with Paolozzi prints and Paul Gell flower paintings, and the oak floor with Oriental rugs. The atmosphere is intimate and relaxed with all the lightness of the barn, but scaled down for cosy evenings, tucked away from the great outdoors.

THE OLD STABLES
GERARD AND SANDI BELLAART

~

The dark purple paint on the arched garden gates hints at Gothick and Oriental inspiration. They open into a jungle-like garden that conceals an eccentric stone building from view; a seventeenth-century stable and brewhouse, one tall and upright, with a steep pantiled roof, beside the lower, single-storey brewhouse with its shallow peg-tiled roof.

They stand near a Gothick folly church with two conical spires ridged like a wedding cake. The Regency Gothick has filtered over the garden wall adding a pointed arch to the door and windows. Unlike any other house in the Somerset village of Rode, the stables have a steeply pitched roof that suggests Dutch origins – a possible legacy from the colony who settled close by to work in woollen mills along the river. Whatever its original function, the building has a long history as stables. In the eighteenth century it belonged to the rectory, and was where the priest kept his horses and perhaps brewed his ale.

Appropriately, for the last 14 years it has been lived in by a Dutchman, Gerard Bellaart and his wife Sandi. As the only Dutchman in Rode he feels quite at home under his indigenous roof. When they bought the building it was in serious need of attention; it had no plumbing, electricity or ground-floor windows – just a water supply. What is now the kitchen was a derelict brewhouse with a dirt floor. The adjoining stables were divided into four stalls with mangers below a loft that was reached by a rickety ladder. As artists, Gerard and Sandi were full of romantic notions. 'We had a rustic idea of just whitewashing it all, having a studio downstairs, then climbing a ladder to live in the loft,' remembers Sandi. 'But, of course, we couldn't live like that. It wasn't practical with all the damp and a spring seeping through the wall.'

While builders worked on their home, Gerard and Sandi camped beside it in a caravan, then spent a year in a studio converted from a double garage. Curing the damp was the main task. The stables had been built without foundations straight on to the earth. An open well by the entrance to the brewhouse

Hidden behind a rampant and productive garden, the eccentric, steep-roofed stables adjoin a single-storey brewhouse, fronted by a conservatory which provides an entrance hall and extra living room

122

ABOVE, *Beneath the arch of an original Gothick window, Sandi has a quiet corner upstairs for bookbinding and restoration*

LEFT, *The kitchen is an alternative living room, an already crowded space where friends gather on squashy sofas and a cushioned window seat around the pine table*

added to the water problem, which was solved, partially, by excavating the whole floor, laying a damp course then tanking the surface with shiny black asphalt. The well remains below ground, bubbling into a pond and filling any holes dug in the garden.

The ground floor of the stables is now a sitting room, reached from the kitchen by an arch cut through the thick stone wall. It is lit by Gothick windows with mullioned glass, copied from the originals, set midway between the loft and ground floor. As the revised plan was to live downstairs and sleep and work upstairs, the hayloft needed expanding. Its floor was lowered and rebuilt with wooden boards which reduced the sitting room height but made enough space for two bedrooms; one for Sandi and Gerard, another for their daughter Duschka, and a small bathroom and studio area. An extra bedroom for their son Damian was squeezed into the roof above, reached by a vertical ladder.

The Bellaarts work in different corners of the house. Gerard is an etcher, and is tucked secretly away in a garden studio. Sandi works upstairs at bookbinding and restoration – an intricate skill she studied for eight years. As a less solitary pursuit she also works in a garden centre in Bath, which suits her passion for plants.

The most striking feature of the stables is how much can be crammed into one rectangular room. There is no false illusion of space created by sparse furnishings. Quite the opposite. It is hard to know where to look first. Both Sandi and Gerard are great collectors of anything ethnic, old or exotic – possessions that reflect a cosmopolitan background. Sandi is Australian and well travelled. She met Gerard in Greece then lived with him in Holland where they still have a flat, 'Just a mattress in Rotterdam'. The Far East has a powerful influence on their style which also has a strong throwback to the 1960s. Gerard admits to being a 1960s relic himself: an outspoken character with a self-deprecating sense of humour; 'an anarchist and atheist,' he claims. Sandi is a gentle foil to his brusqueness. Although anglicized, lapses into Dutch give a foreign intonation to her soft voice. She feels drawn to anything ethnic and hand crafted. 'She likes the Far East because their people are further removed from plastic than we are,' explains Gerard.

The interior reflects an artist's eye for invention. 'We never have any money so we have to improvise,' says Sandi. It was easy to find junk shop bargains 14 years ago: the arched double doors in the kitchen and sitting room came from a reclamation centre; the black spiral staircase tucked in a corner of the sitting room from a fairground. 'It was covered in cut out rabbits, but we took those off.' Shelves stacked with art books have been fitted into a wall recess – a simple construction of wooden planks laid between stone bookends, dismantled from an old garden seat.

The thick walls give each window a deep stone sill. Some have one simple curtain of oatmeal linen that matches the stone frames, others are bare, letting their Gothick tracery add to the decoration. Mirrors at right angles to a window throw extra light into the room, which after dark is lit by lanterns and candles. A round window looking out over the fields has been inscribed with a Tibetan mantra, emphasizing the ethnic atmosphere. The backdrop of white walls and glossy-black floor sets off the rich colour and textures of accumulated treasures. Oriental carpets cover walls and floors, Kashmiri shawls are draped on sofas heaped with tapestry cushions. Cats curl around a terrarium fish tank that sits on a carved Indian table. A cast-iron printing press stands at one end. Someday they plan to have a private press, publishing books printed by Gerard and bound by Sandi. It keeps company with a carved oak marriage chest and a curious object known as 'The Folly' – an eccentric sixteenth-century what-not, belonging to Sandi's artist grandmother who had long abandoned it to spiders and birds.

A more recent acquisition is a woodburning stove installed at the far end of the stables. 'We had to sell a carpet to pay for it but it's the first time we've really been warm.' The stove stands in the hearth of an unsuccessful Gothick fireplace that was put in during the conversion. It refused to draw, smoked horribly and caused a drama when a beam inside the chimney caught fire.

The kitchen is about half the size of the sitting room but appears to be more of an alternative living space. The practical side is obvious – colourful plates, glass jars, canisters, pots and pans cover the white walls and pale-pine cupboards, but there is a striking lack of gadgets or concessions to man-made conveniences. It is definitely a room for people. Friends call in for meals, fresh coffee, cake and conversation around the kitchen table, sitting on squashy sofas or a cushioned window seat. A round pine table top rests on an antique sewing machine base. The surface has been painted with a clear white varnish from Holland that gives a limed effect. 'It's supposed to have one coat, but the cat landed on the wet paint, so I had to cover the footprints. One thing about this place is that everything is quite rustic, not perfectly done at all,' says Sandi.

Perhaps because of this, the atmosphere is immediately hospitable and cosmopolitan. In the kitchen, Gothick style verges on the Moorish, suggested by onion-domed arches in a blue stained-glass window and cast-iron fretwork over the door, which also hides the gas stove. The black and terracotta coloured lino floor is a recent addition, replacing the asphalt which drenched the Oriental rugs as a result of the rising

damp. 'Black isn't very practical but we wanted it to match the floor next door,' explains Sandi. Hidden in the 'back room' are the washing machine, fridge and other necessities, 'all rotting away nicely in the damp'. Originally, they stood in an open-sided lean-to along the north side of both buildings, facing fields and the Bellaarts' vegetable garden, but the cold and howling winds forced them to seal the frame using windows from a local reclamation centre. 'We discovered they came from a lunatic asylum, so I wonder what sort of karma came with them?'

To Sandi, plants are as precious as junk shop finds. 'We've collected pieces over the years. Now there is no more room inside, so we collect plants instead.' Her favourite part of the house is a conservatory added unobtrusively in front of the kitchen four years ago. It is a simple, south-facing lean-to that adds to the light and size of the kitchen and gives Sandi a place to grow all the exotic plants she loves. Here her bougainvillea, oleander, datura, abutilon and ginger plants thrive in pots and a bed dug out of the ground.

She began the transformation outside by turning the cobbled yard into a symbolic garden. But, according to country lore, 'the most symbolic plants were the kind of herbs that didn't look marvellous all year around'. She then succumbed to her passion for exotic plants – a scheme that was ruined by a bitter winter that killed 30 tender shrubs. Now the planting has been replanned to suit the climate and clay soil. A prolific combination of trees, shrubs, bulbs and perennials grow in terracotta pots, old tin pig-buckets and large curving borders. Her tastes and ideas change constantly, calling for more and more plants to be squeezed into harmonized groups.

The garden is small but filling it to capacity gives an illusion of extra space. Unusual trees add to the dense jungle that grows up in summer; a twisted willow (*Salix* 'Tortuosa') thrives with its roots sprawled into a drain, an oversized white leaf acer (*Acer negundo*), a red leaved Judas tree (*Cercis siliquastrum*) and a Morello cherry tree. Against the stable wall, a productive fig tree, passion flower, clematis and evergreen climbers add colour to the mottled gold of the Somerset stone.

In summer, the front door into the living room stays open, adding sunlight and exotic garden scents to the cosmopolitan interior

INDEX